NO-BAKE DESSERTS

NO-FAT LOW-FAT
DESSERTS

100 LIGHT & FRUITY RECIPES

Simona Hill

southwater

This edition is published by Southwater
an imprint of
Anness Publishing Ltd
Hermes House
88–89 Blackfriars Road
London SE1 8HA
tel. 020 7401 2077; fax 020 7633 9499

www.southwaterbooks.com; www.annesspublishing.com

If you like the images in this book and would like to investigate using them for publishing, promotions or advertising, please visit our website www.practicalpictures.com for more information.

UK distributor: Book Trade Services
tel. 0116 275 9086; fax 0116 275 9090
uksales@booktradeservices.com
exportsales@booktradeservices.com

North American distributor: National Book Network
tel. 301 459 3366; fax 301 429 5746
www.nbnbooks.com

Australian distributor: Pan Macmillan Australia
tel. 1300 135 113; fax 1300 135 103
customer.service@macmillan.com.au

New Zealand distributor: David Bateman Ltd
tel. (09) 415 7664; fax (09) 415 8892

Publisher: Joanna Lorenz
Editorial Director: Helen Sudell
Editor: Simona Hill
Production Controller: Christine Ni

Recipes: Catherine Atkinson, Alex Barker,
Michelle Berriedale-Johnson, Angela Boggiano, Janet Brinkworth,
Carla Capalbo, Jacqueline Clark, Frances Cleary, Carol Clements,
Roz Denny, Patrizia Diemling, Nicola Diggins, Joanna Farrow,
Christine France, Sarah Gates, Shirley Gill, Rosamund Grant,
Carole Handslip, Deh-Ta Hsiung, Shehzad Husain,
Sheila Kimberley, Gilly Love, Sue Maggs, Maggie Mayhew,
Maggie Parnell, Anne Sheasby, Liz Trigg, Laura Washburn,
Steven Wheeler, Kate Whiteman, Elizabeth Wolf-Cohen
and Jeni Wright

Photographers: William Lingwood, Karl Adamson,
Edward Allwright, David Armstrong, Steve Baxter, James Duncan,
Michelle Garrett, Amanda Heywood, David Jordan, Don Last,
Patrick McLeavey, Michael Michaels and Thomas Odulate

Front cover shows Raspberry Sorbet – for recipe, see page 119

ETHICAL TRADING POLICY
Because of our ongoing ecological investment programme, you, as our customer, can have the pleasure and reassurance of knowing that a tree is being cultivated on your behalf to naturally replace the materials used to make the book you are holding. For further information about this scheme, go to www.annesspublishing.com/trees

© Anness Publishing Ltd 2011

Previously published as part of a larger volume,
The Ultimate Fat-Free Dessert Cookbook

PUBLISHER'S NOTE
Although the advice and information in this book are believed to be accurate and true at the time of going to press, neither the authors nor the publisher can accept any legal responsibility or liability for any errors or omissions that may have been made nor for any inaccuracies nor for any loss, harm or injury that comes about from following instructions or advice in this book.

NOTES
Bracketed terms are intended for American readers.
For all recipes, quantities are given in both metric and imperial measures and, where appropriate, in standard cups and spoons. Follow one set of measures, but not a mixture, because they are not interchangeable.
Standard spoon and cup measures are level. 1 tsp = 5ml, 1 tbsp = 15ml, 1 cup = 250ml/8fl oz.
Australian standard tablespoons are 20ml. Australian readers should use 3 tsp in place of 1 tbsp for measuring small quantities.
American pints are 16fl oz/2 cups. American readers should use 20fl oz/2.5 cups in place of 1 pint when measuring liquids.
Electric oven temperatures in this book are for conventional ovens. When using a fan oven, the temperature will probably need to be reduced by about 10–20°C/20–40°F. Since ovens vary, you should check with your manufacturer's instruction book for guidance.
The nutritional analysis given for each recipe is calculated per portion (i.e. serving or item), unless otherwise stated. If the recipe gives a range, such as Serves 4–6, then the nutritional analysis will be for the smaller portion size, i.e. 6 servings.
The analysis does not include optional items, such as ingredients added to taste.
Medium (US large) eggs are used unless otherwise stated.

CONTENTS

INTRODUCTION

All too often, dessert is the downfall of the person trying to follow a low-fat diet, particularly for those of us who are sweet-toothed. After a sensible starter and a healthy main course composed of grilled fish or chicken and fresh vegetables, there's an almost irresistible temptation to feel an entitlement to a portion of pudding.

The good news is that you can still have dessert, and every day too, if you are careful with your food choices and strict with your portion sizes. You don't have to give up lovely, luscious sweets – provided you stick to the low-fat recipes in this book. Carefully designed to fit into a healthy, lighter diet, each has no more than 5g of fat per portion, and many of the recipes have fewer than 200 calories, making them a perfect choice for dieters.

The secret of eating for good health is making sure that your diet has a sound nutritional balance. Cutting down on fat but increasing sugar is not the solution, so while these puddings bring a little sweetness into our days, many of them do so by using small amounts of honey or the natural sugars present in fresh fruits.

We all know we should be eating more fruit – it is recommended that we eat five portions of fresh fruit or vegetables each day – so fresh fruit desserts score on a variety of levels, not only supplying sweetness, but also contributing fibre,

essential vitamins and minerals. Fruits offer a perfect food package, giving freshness to our meals, which are essential in a well-balanced diet. The addition of different food colours to the dessert plate adds to its appeal, The recipes in this book make full use of the wonderfully abundant choice of fruits that are available through the summer months, sweet blueberries, tart blackcurrants, delicious strawberries, raspberries, and blackberries as well as a whole array of tropical fruits, which are at their most economical and flavourful at this time of year. Included too, are desserts that make the most of year-round fruits, such as apples, oranges and bananas.

We are also lucky to have available lots of delicious, lighter alternatives to high-fat ingredients such as cream – so even classic rich dishes can be lightened quite easily, either by substituting a high-fat dairy product with a low-fat one, or by simply choosing a different serving accompaniment. You'll find that, after a while, your tastes will change, and in many cases you will actually prefer the lighter, fresher flavours of low-fat desserts to some of the over-rich alternatives.

So whether you are aiming to eat less fat in order to lose weight, or just adopt a permanent healthy approach to food, this book will help you do so without giving up the sweet things in life.

BELOW: Summer berries are full of natural sugar, but have barely any fat. Serve them with low-fat yogurt.

BELOW: Apricot parcels make the most of fresh apricots, which are only available for a short season.

ABOVE: Pancake batter contains little fat, and can be fried with minimal oil in the pan. Serve with fruit compote or syrup.

ABOVE: Meringues contain hardly any fat. They taste divine eaten with summer fruit and low-fat yogurt.

MAKING DESSERTS THE FAT-FREE WAY

Dessert, to many people, means indulgent puddings and pies made with butter, sugar and flour as the basis, then served with cream, custard or ice cream. Choosing low-fat alternatives does mean having to alter your expectations of what constitutes dessert, but does not necessarily mean that you have to eat tiny portion sizes. It is perfectly possible to have a luscious, creamy sweet, when all the while, the constituents are fat-free or low in fat.

Many dessert ingredients are available in reduced-fat or very low-fat forms. In every supermarket you'll find a huge array of such products, such as milk, cream, yogurt, hard and soft cheeses and fromage frais, reduced-fat sweet or chocolate biscuits; low-fat, half-fat or very low-fat spreads; as well as reduced-fat ready-made desserts. Some ingredients work better than others in cooking, but often a simple substitution will spell success. In a crumb crust, for instance, reduced-fat cookies work just as well as classic digestives (graham crackers).

Some of the most delicious desserts are based upon fruit. Serve fresh in a salad or compote, and there's absolutely no need to introduce fats. The secret is to choose ingredients that are ripe because then they are at their most flavourful. Fruit that is barbecued, such as bananas or pineapple, has an intense sweet flavour that needs no accompaniment. Barbecues are synonymous with summer and there are plenty of recipes included to help you make the most of outdoor cooking. Alternately, if you are making pancakes, or pan-frying fruit such as bananas or pineapple rings, you can get away with using a fine mist of spray oil, especially if you use a non-stick pan. A one-second spray of sunflower oil (about 1ml) has 4.6 Kcals/18.8 kJ and just over half the fat of conventional cooking oil. Spray oil is perfect for lightly greasing dishes too.

When seeking inspiration for the dessert course remember that there are plenty of ingredients that naturally contain very little fat. Rice, flour, rolled oats, bread and cornflakes can all be used to make puddings and toppings, and there's no fat in alcohol, sugar or honey, although you may wish to restrict these for other reasons! Meringues are among the most popular puddings – topped with fresh fruit and yogurt or fromage frais, they are irresistible to eat and look great. The recipes in this book also feature pastries, custards, ice creams and sorbets, all of which can be made surprisingly low in fat. Filo pastry is a perfect substitute for shortcrust for those who like a dessert with added crunch. This light and airy pastry is brushed with melted low-fat butter or margarine and stacked and layered with fruit to create a perfect sweet, that makes an irresistible finale to a special meal. Sorbet, too, is incredibly low in fat, but big on flavour, and adds the sweet taste that dieters often crave to finish off a meal.

Spices and extracts add plenty of additional flavour to desserts. Vanilla is a classic ingredient for desserts, and if you extract the seed from the bean, the taste will be intense and pure. Presentation of the dessert is everything and decorations like rose petals, mint leaves or curls of pared citrus rind add to the appearance of the presentation as well as helping to stimulate the appetite.

FACTS ABOUT FATS

We all know we need to cut down on the amount of fat we eat – it would be difficult to live in the developed world and be unaware of that fact – but before making changes in our diet, it may be helpful to find out a bit more about the fats that we eat: some types are believed to be less harmful than others.

Fats are essential for the proper functioning of the body. However, we need the right kind of fat and the right amount. The average Western diet contains far too much saturated fat, which leads to obesity, heart problems and strokes. The daily recommended maximum amount of calories that should come from fat is between 30 and 35 per cent. Many of us obtain more than 40 per cent of our calories from fat, often in the form of treats, desserts and pastries.

Fats in our food are made up of different types of fatty acids and glycerol. Fats may be saturated or unsaturated, with unsaturated fat further categorized as mono-unsaturated or polyunsaturated.

BELOW: Butter is a saturated fat that gives food flavour, but should be restricted if you are following a low-fat diet.

SATURATED FATS

To appreciate the difference between saturated and unsaturated fatty acids, it is necessary to understand a little about their molecular structure. Put very simply, fatty acids are made up of chains of carbon atoms. A common analogy is to liken them to a string of beads. Unlike beads, however, which are linked to each other, the carbon atoms are able to link up – or bond – with one or more other atoms.

In a saturated fat, all these potential linkages have been made: the carbon atoms are linked to each other and each is further linked to two hydrogen atoms. No further linkages are possible, and the fat is therefore said to be saturated.

Saturated fat is mainly found in foods of animal origin: meat and dairy products such as butter, which is solid at room temperature. However, there are also some saturated fats of vegetable origin, notably coconut oil and palm oil. Palm oil is the main vegetable oil used in hard margarines. It is better to avoid both.

BELOW: Unsaturated fats are liquid at room temperature, and are better for us, but still need to be restricted.

UNSATURATED FATS

Unsaturated fatty acids differ from saturated fatty acids in their structure – not all of the linkages or bonds are complete. Some of the carbon atoms may be joined to each other by a double bond. Depending on how many double bonds there are, the fatty acid is described as mono-unsaturated (one double bond) or polyunsaturated (many double bonds). As a general rule, unsaturated fats are more healthy than saturated fats.

MONO-UNSATURATED FATS

These are found in foods such as olive oil, rapeseed oil, some nuts, oily fish and avocado pears. Mono-unsaturated fats are believed to be neutral, neither raising or lowering blood cholesterol levels. People who live in Mediterranean countries eat a diet that contains mostly mono-unsaturated fats. In addition, their diet contains a high proportion of fruit and vegetables, which are high in antioxidants. This could explain why there is such a low incidence of heart disease in these countries.

POLYUNSATURATED FATS

There are two types of polyunsaturated fats. The first (omega 6) is found in vegetable and seed oils, such as sunflower or almond oil, and the second (omega 3) comes from oily fish, green leaves and some seed oils, including rapeseed or canola oil. Polyunsaturated fats are liquid at room temperature. These are the best types of fat to eat and are essential to maintain movement in joints, keep skin supple, provide a reserve of energy for the body, keep us warm and, balance our hormones keep cells healthy.

• Use heavy or non-stick pans – so you won't need as much fat for cooking.

• Use good quality cookware that doesn't need greasing before use, or line the pan with non-stick paper and only grease very lightly before filling.

• Look out for non-stick coated fabric sheeting. This reusable material will not stick and is amazingly versatile. It can be cut to size and used to line cake tins, baking sheets or frying pans. It is heat resistant to 290°C/550°F and microwave safe.

• Bake fruit in a loosely sealed parcel of baking paper, moistening it with wine, fruit juice or liqueur, not butter.

QUICK TIPS FOR FAT-FREE COOKING

• When grilling fruit, the naturally high moisture content means that it is often unnecessary to add fat. If the fruit looks a bit dry, brush lightly and sparingly with a polyunsaturated oil such as sunflower oil.

• Fruit cooked in the microwave seldom needs additional fat; add spices for extra colour and flavour.

• Poach fresh fruit in natural juice or syrup – there's no need to add any fat.

• Become an expert at cooking with filo pastry. Of itself, filo is extremely low in fat, and if you brush the sheets sparingly with melted low-fat spread, it can be used to make delicious puddings that will not significantly damage a low-fat diet.

• Avoid cooking with chocolate, which is high in fat. If you can't bear to abandon your favourite flavour, use reduced-fat cocoa powder instead.

• Get to know the full range of low- or reduced-fat products, including yogurt, crème fraîche and fromage frais. Low-fat yogurt can be used for making sauces, but needs to be treated with care as it is liable to curdle when heated. Stabilize it by stirring in a little cornflour (cornstarch), mixed to a paste with water or skimmed milk.

• Use skimmed milk rather than whole milk in puddings and batters. The flavour will be slightly less creamy.

TRANS-FATS

When vegetable oils are used in the manufacture of soft margarine, they have to be hardened artificially. During this process, the composition of some of the unsaturated fatty acids changes. In the body, these altered or "trans" fatty acids are treated like saturated fats, so, although an oil such as sunflower oil may be high in polyunsaturated fatty acids, the same is not necessarily true of a margarine made from that oil.

Polyunsaturated fats lower cholesterol levels. Although unsaturated fats are more healthy than saturated ones, most experts agree that what matters more is that we all reduce our total intake of fat.

LOW-FAT SPREADS IN COOKING

Some low-fat spreads can safely be substituted for butter or margarine in baked puddings, but others are only suitable for spreading. The limiting factor is the amount of water in the product. Very low-fat spreads achieve levels of fat of around 20 per cent by virtue of their high water content and cannot be melted successfully. Spreads with a fat content of

around 40 per cent are suitable for spreading and for some cooking methods. Product packets contain guidance.

When using low-fat spreads for cooking, the fat may behave slightly differently to full-fat products such as butter or margarine. Be prepared to experiment a little. When heating low-fat spreads, never let them get too hot. Always use a heavy pan over a low heat to avoid the product burning, spitting or spoiling, and stir all the time.

BELOW: Whipped cream adds fat to desserts. Use low-fat yogurt in its place.

Desserts made using reduced fat spreads do not keep as well as those made using butter because of the lower fat content.

LOW-FAT ACCOMPANIMENTS

Low-fat yogurt, Greek (US strained plain) yogurt, frozen yogurt, sorbet, low-fat ice cream and low-fat custard all make suitable accompaniments to desserts. Remember to include the extra calories in your calorie count, though.

BELOW: Greek-style yogurt is thick and creamy and available with 0 per cent fat.

A GUIDE TO INGREDIENTS

The dessert ingredients in these recipes will be familiar to you, and you may find that you have many of the basics already in your storecupboard.

FRUIT

Used in every recipe in this book as a flavouring, or a main ingredient, fruit is naturally sweet and contains little or no fat, and for those reasons is perfect to incorporate into desserts for those following a low-fat eating plan. It's also light on the palate and adds sweetness, sharpness and flavour to desserts. Fruit adds colour and texture to dishes making desserts look appealing and smell deliciously fresh. Fruit is also fantastically versatile. Most can be eaten whole and raw, a perfect package of sweetness and energy to eat on the go, or it can be stewed and puréed to eat as they are or as an accompaniment to a dessert, as well as to form the basis for crumbles. They can be filled and baked, peeled, stoned (pitted), sliced and diced for all manner of dessert bases. For best results,

BELOW: Flavourful summer berries are perfect for low-fat desserts.

ABOVE: Butter, sugar, eggs and flour are the basis for most desserts.

and the most economical options, buy fruit when it is naturally in season, because it will have the best flavour and will cost less. Fruits that are available all year round such as apples, bananas and oranges are used as well as those that have a short season such as berry fruits, grapes, rhubarb, melon, peaches and nectarines, and tropical fruits such as kiwi, mango, pineapple and papaya.

BELOW: Orchard fruits are available all year round and do not contain any fat.

Dried fruits, such as sultanas, raisins, dates and dried pineapple cubes, are used in some recipes so worthwhile storing.

STORECUPBOARD INGREDIENTS

Flour, sugar, milk, eggs and butter are the base for many cakes, puddings and dessert toppings, but traditional combinations of these ingredients make for desserts that are high in fat and sugar. By using skimmed (very low-fat) milk in place of whole milk and replacing butter with low-fat spread or oil, and by reducing the overall quantity of these ingredients in the dessert, it is still possible to make traditional-style desserts that are healthier and lower in fat and still taste delicious.

Sugar does not contain fat, but healthy guidelines suggest that it should be eaten in moderation. Many types of sugar are incorporated into the recipes in this book, with each adding flavour notes to the dish, such as muscovado (raw) sugar, adding caramel notes, and icing (confectioners') sugar adding intense sweetness. Other ingredients, such as rolled oats, pudding rice also contain little fat and are good base ingredients for low-fat desserts.

Also used in smaller quantities are some higher fat products, which add distinct flavour. Unsalted nuts such as flaked (sliced) almonds, pistachio nuts, ground almond and hazelnuts, add density as well as well as nutritional value. Sesame and poppy seeds are also beneficial and add flavour to some desserts.

Pastry is high in saturated fats and often strictly off-limits for those following a low-fat diet, but if pastry is a weakness, you can still have it in moderation. Filo pastry is a wafer thin pastry, made of flour and water. The fat content is added to it at the baking stage, usually when melted butter is brushed on to each layer before another layer is added. Relatively low in calories in comparison to other pastries, filo pastry is a good choice for those who crave desserts made with pastry, as long as you control carefully the amount of fat added. Keep a packet in the freezer.

Low-fat dessert fillings can be made from mincemeat and marzipan – perfect when luxury and flavour are the order of day, and combined with fruits, these ingredients will go a long way.

ABOVE: The seeds of the vanilla bean are light and sweet in taste.

ABOVE: Ground ginger, cinnamon and nutmeg are all useful additions to dessert.

FLAVOURINGS

As well as being the main flavour and bulk ingredient in many recipes, fruits also provide additional flavouring. Citrus zests add sharpness as well as flavour, and orange- and rose-flower waters provide scent and sweetness to desserts. Honey adds subtle sweetness as well as flavour, while the addition of coffee will create strong flavour notes.

In addition, many spices add pronounced and complementary flavours to fruits. Cinnamon, mixed (apple pie) spice, ground ginger and cloves provide

warmth and strength to other foods. Black pepper adds heat and chat masala is a tangy and hot spice. Vanilla extract, nutmeg and ginger can all provide key flavour notes to desserts.

Jam, redcurrant jelly and dry unsweetened shredded coconut are all suitable additions, where a little quantity adds large amounts of flavour.

DRINKS

Alcohol adds intense flavour to dessert, as well as luxury. It is relatively high in calories but is used in small quantities. The alcohol content will evaporate during

the cooking process, leaving a warming flavour. Spirits such as brandy, rum, port and vodka, liqueurs, as well as red and white wines are all included in these recipes. If the alcohol is not baked, then the recipes are unsuitable to serve to children. Simply omit the alcohol or substitute a fruit juice in its place. Fruit juices such as pineapple, orange, apple and grape juice are incorporated into some recipes, providing liquid flavour. Choose unsweetened varieties and for the most intense flavour, choose a juice that is not made from concentrate for best results.

BELOW: Nuts contain good fats, but should be added to desserts in moderation.

BELOW: Alcohol can be added to some desserts in very small quantities.

BELOW: Fruit juices add flavour to a recipe and contain no fat.

HOT FRUIT PUDDINGS AND DESSERTS

There's something about a piping hot pudding that appeals to our sense of nostalgia. This chapter presents filling sweet treats that hark back to yesteryear – Blueberry Buckle and Rhubarb Spiral Cobbler are old-fashioned puds that are hard to resist. Such hot desserts are deliciously comforting as well as tasty. The aroma of sweet goods baking is a pleasure to savour, even for those of us following a low-fat eating plan. Included too are light and flavourful desserts incorporating many kinds of fruit, from Nectarines with Marzipan and Yogurt to Caribbean Bananas, plus there are plenty of ideas for making the most of the barbecue.

 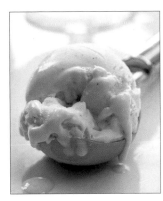  

BAKED APPLES IN HONEY AND LEMON

—

A classic combination of flavours in a healthy and old-fashioned family pudding. This dessert is quick to put together. Serve warm, with skimmed-milk custard, if you like.

3 With a cannelle knife or a sharp knife with a narrow pointed blade, cut lines through the apple skin at intervals. Stand the apples in an ovenproof dish.

4 In a small bowl, mix the honey, lemon rind, juice and low-fat spread.

INGREDIENTS
4 cooking apples
15ml/1 tbsp clear honey
grated rind and juice of 1 lemon
15ml/1 tbsp low-fat spread
low-fat-custard, to serve (optional)

SERVES 4

NUTRITIONAL NOTES
Per portion:

Energy	78Kcals/326kJ
Fat, total	1.7g
Saturated fat	0.37g
Cholesterol	0.2mg
Fibre	2.4g

1 Preheat the oven to 180°C/350°F/ Gas 4.

2 Carefully remove the core from each of the apples, but do not cut right through to the base or the filling will run out of the base when the apples are baked.

5 Spoon the mixture into the apples and cover the dish with foil or a lid.

6 Bake for 40–45 minutes, or until the apples are tender. Serve with the custard, if you like.

SPICED PEAR AND BLUEBERRY PARCELS

This combination makes a delicious dessert for a summer's evening when pears are at their most flavourful. This dessert can be cooked on a barbecue or in the oven.

INGREDIENTS
4 firm, ripe pears
30ml/2 tbsp lemon juice
25g/¹/₂ oz/1 tbsp low-fat spread, melted
150g/5oz/1¹/₄ cups blueberries
50g/2oz/4 tbsp light muscovado
(brown) sugar
freshly ground black pepper

SERVES 4

NUTRITIONAL NOTES
Per portion:

Energy	146Kcals/614kJ
Fat, total	1.8g
Saturated fat	0.37g
Cholesterol	0.2mg
Fibre	4g

1 Prepare the barbecue or preheat the oven to 200°C/400°F/Gas 6.

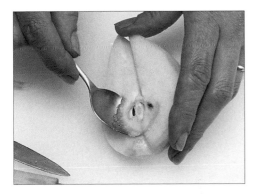

2 Peel the pears and cut them in half lengthways. Scoop out the core. Brush with lemon juice, to stop the pears browning.

VARIATION
Instead of blueberries, try diced nectarines, if you like.

---

3 Cut eight squares of kitchen foil, each large enough to wrap a pear. Place two together. Brush the top layer with spread.

4 Place two pear halves on each kitchen foil stack, cut side upwards. Gather the foil around them, to hold them level.

5 Mix the blueberries and sugar together and spoon it on top of the pears. Sprinkle with black pepper.

6 Wrap the foil over and cook for 20–25 minutes on a hot barbecue or in the oven.

STRAWBERRY AND APPLE CRUMBLE

—

A high-fibre, low-fat version of the classic apple crumble. Fresh or frozen raspberries
can be used instead of strawberries.

4 Tip the mixture into a 1.2 litre/2 pint/5
cup ovenproof dish.

5 To make the crumble combine the flour
and oats in a bowl and mix in the low-fat
spread with a fork, or use your fingertips,
until it resembles fine crumbs.

6 Sprinkle the crumble evenly over
the fruit.

7 Bake for 40–45 minutes, until golden
brown and bubbling. Serve warm, with
custard or yogurt, if you like.

INGREDIENTS

150g/5oz/1¼ cups strawberries, hulled
450g/1lb cooking apples, peeled, cored
and sliced
30ml/2 tbsp caster (superfine) sugar
2.5ml/½ tsp ground cinnamon
30ml/2 tbsp orange juice
low-fat custard or yogurt, to serve (optional)

FOR THE CRUMBLE

45ml/3 tbsp wholemeal
(whole-wheat) flour
50g/2oz/⅔ cup rolled oats
30ml/2 tbsp low-fat spread

SERVES 4

1 Preheat the oven to 180°C/350°F/
Gas 4.

2 Halve the strawberries.

3 Toss together the apples, strawberries,
sugar, cinnamon and orange juice.

NUTRITIONAL NOTES
Per portion:

Energy	173Kcals/729kJ
Fat, total	3.9g
Saturated fat	0.85g
Cholesterol	0.4mg
Fibre	3.5g

BLUEBERRY BUCKLE

This fruity dessert is an American speciality. It is a single layer cake, traditionally with a heavy batter. This lighter version can be served with low-fat Greek yogurt, if you like.

INGREDIENTS

30ml/2 tbsp low-fat spread, plus extra
for greasing
175g/6oz/3/4 cup sugar
1 egg
2.5ml/1/2 tsp vanilla extract
225g/8oz/2 cups plain (all-purpose) flour
10ml/2 tsp baking powder (soda)
2.5ml/1/2 tsp salt
175ml/6fl oz/3/4 cup skimmed
(very low-fat) milk
450g/1lb/4 cups fresh blueberries
low-fat Greek (US strained plain) yogurt,
to serve (optional)

FOR THE TOPPING

115g/4oz/2/3 cup soft light brown sugar
50g/2oz/1/2 cup plain (all-purpose) flour
2.5ml/1/2 tsp salt
2.5ml/1/2 tsp mixed (apple pie) spice
45ml/3 tbsp low-fat spread
10ml/2 tsp skimmed (very low-fat) milk
5ml/1 tsp vanilla extract

SERVES 8

1 Preheat the oven to 190°C/375°F/Gas 5. Grease a 23cm/9in round baking dish.

2 Beat the low-fat spread with the sugar. Add the egg and vanilla. Sift over the flour, baking powder and salt, stirring in alternately with the milk.

3 Pour the mixture into the prepared dish and sprinkle over the blueberries.

4 To make the topping, mix the brown sugar, flour, salt and mixed spice in a bowl. Rub in the spread until the mixture resembles coarse crumbs.

NUTRITIONAL NOTES

Per portion:

Energy	338Kcals/1432kJ
Fat, total	4.9g
Saturated fat	1.14g
Cholesterol	25.1mg
Fibre	2.1g

5 Mix the milk and vanilla together. Drizzle over the topping. Stir with a fork.

6 Sprinkle the topping over the blueberries. Bake for 45 minutes, or until a skewer inserted in the centre comes out clean. Serve warm, with yogurt.

CORNFLAKE-TOPPED PEACH BAKE

—

With just a few store cupboard ingredients, this golden, cornflake-crusted, family
pudding can be rustled up in next to no time.

INGREDIENTS

415g/14¹/2 oz can peach slices in juice
30ml/2 tbsp sultanas (golden raisins)
1 cinnamon stick
strip of pared orange rind
30ml/2 tbsp low-fat spread
50g/2oz/1¹/2 cups cornflakes
10ml/2 tsp sesame seeds

SERVES 4

1 Preheat the oven to 200°C/400°F/
Gas 6.

2 Drain the peaches, reserving the juice
in a small pan. Arrange the peach slices
in a shallow ovenproof dish.

3 Add the sultanas, cinnamon stick and
orange rind to the juice and bring to the
boil. Lower the heat and simmer, for
3–4 minutes, to reduce the liquid by half.
Remove the cinnamon stick and rind and
spoon the syrup over the peaches.

4 Melt the low-fat spread in a small pan,
stir in the cornflakes and sesame seeds.

5 Spread the cornflake mixture over the
fruit. Bake for 15–20 minutes, or until the
topping is crisp and golden. Serve hot.

NUTRITIONAL NOTES
Per portion:

Energy	150Kcals/633kJ
Fat, total	4.6g
Saturated fat	1g
Cholesterol	0.5mg
Fibre	1.3g

RHUBARB SPIRAL COBBLER

The tangy taste of rhubarb stewed with sugar and orange juice combines perfectly with the
ginger spice in this unusual Swiss roll topping.

INGREDIENTS
675g/1¹/₂ lb rhubarb, sliced
45ml/3 tbsp unsweetened orange juice
75g/3oz/6 tbsp caster (superfine) sugar
200g/7oz/1³/₄ cups self-raising
(self-rising) flour
about 250ml/8fl oz/1 cup low-fat natural
(plain) yogurt
grated rind of 1 orange
30ml/2 tbsp demerara (raw) sugar
5ml/1 tsp ground ginger

SERVES 4

1 Preheat the oven to 200°C/400°F/
Gas 6.

2 Mix the rhubarb, orange juice and
50g/2oz/4 tbsp of the caster sugar in a
pan. Cover and cook over a low heat for
10 minutes or until tender.

3 Tip the fruit into an ovenproof dish.

NUTRITIONAL NOTES
Per portion:

Energy	320Kcals/1343kJ
Fat, total	1.2g
Saturated fat	0.34g
Cholesterol	2mg
Fibre	3.92g

4 To make the topping, mix the flour and
remaining caster sugar in a bowl, then
stir in enough of the yogurt to bind to a
soft dough.

5 Roll out the dough on a floured surface
to a 25cm/10in square.

6 Mix the orange rind, demerara sugar
and ginger in a small bowl, then sprinkle
this over the dough.

7 Roll up the dough quite tightly.

8 Cut the roll into 10 slices. Arrange
over the stewed rhubarb.

9 Bake for 20–25 minutes, or until the
spirals are well risen and golden brown.
Serve warm, with yogurt if you like.

VARIATION
Substitute halved plums, sliced
nectarines or peaches for the rhubarb.

BARBECUED BANANAS WITH SPICY VANILLA SPREAD

Baked bananas are a must for the barbecue – they're such an easy dessert because they bake
in their own skins and need no preparation at all.

3 Meanwhile, split the cardamom pods
and remove the seeds. Place the seeds in
a mortar and crush lightly with a pestle.

4 Split the vanilla pod lengthways and
scrape out the tiny seeds. Mix with the
cardamom seeds, orange rind, brandy,
sugar and spread, to make a thick paste.

5 Wearing oven gloves, carefully split
the skin of each banana, open out slightly
and spoon in a little of the paste. Serve at
once, while the paste melts.

INGREDIENTS
4 bananas
6 green cardamom pods (beans)
1 vanilla pod (bean)
finely grated rind of 1 small orange
30ml/2 tbsp brandy
60ml/4 tbsp light muscovado
(brown) sugar
45ml/3 tbsp low-fat spread

SERVES 4

1 Preheat the barbecue.

2 Place the bananas, in their skins, on
the hot barbecue and leave for 6–8
minutes, turning occasionally, until they
turn brownish-black.

COOK'S TIP
If making this recipe for children, use
orange juice instead of the brandy or, if
the fat content is no object, drizzle the
cooked bananas with melted chocolate.

NUTRITIONAL NOTES
Per portion:

Energy	215Kcals/900kJ
Fat, total	4.9g
Saturated fat	1.22g
Cholesterol	0.7mg
Fibre	1.1g

HOT SPICED BANANAS

Baking bananas in a rum and fruit syrup makes for a tropical dessert with negligible
fat and maximum flavour, that's perfect for a hot summer's day.

INGREDIENTS
low-fat spread, for greasing
6 ripe bananas
200g/7oz/generous 1 cup light brown sugar
*250ml/8fl oz/1 cup unsweetened
pineapple juice*
120ml/4fl oz/¹/2 cup dark rum
2 cinnamon sticks
12 whole cloves

SERVES 6

NUTRITIONAL NOTES
Per portion:

Energy	290Kcals/1215kJ
Fat, total	0.3g
Saturated fat	0.11g
Cholesterol	0mg
Fibre	1.1g

4 Add the rum, cinnamon sticks and
cloves. Bring to the boil, then remove the
pan from heat.

5 Pour the hot liquid over the bananas.
Bake for 25–30 minutes until the bananas
are hot and tender. Serve while still hot.

1 Preheat the oven to 180°C/350°F/Gas 4.
Grease a 23cm/9in baking dish.

2 Peel the bananas and cut them
diagonally into 2.5cm/1in pieces.
Arrange the banana evenly over the base
of the baking dish.

3 Mix the sugar and pineapple juice in a
pan. Heat gently until the sugar has
dissolved, stirring occasionally.

RUM AND RAISIN BANANAS

For this recipe choose almost-ripe bananas with evenly coloured skins, either all yellow
or just green at the tips, so that they keep their shape while cooking.

INGREDIENTS
40g/1¹/2 oz/¹/4 cup raisins
75ml/5 tbsp dark rum
15ml/1 tbsp low-fat spread
60ml/4 tbsp soft light brown sugar
4 ripe bananas, peeled and
halved lengthways
1.5ml/¹/4 tsp grated nutmeg
1.5ml/¹/4 tsp ground cinnamon
15ml/1 tbsp flaked (slivered)
almonds, toasted
low-fat fromage frais or low-fat vanilla
ice cream, to serve (optional)

SERVES 4

1 Put the raisins in a bowl and pour over
the rum. Leave to soak for 30 minutes.

2 Melt the spread in a frying pan, add
the sugar and stir until it dissolves.

3 Add the bananas. Cook for a few
minutes until tender, turning once.

4 Sprinkle the spices over the bananas,
then pour over the rum and raisins.
Carefully set alight using a long-handled
match; stir gently to mix.

5 Sprinkle over the flaked almonds and
serve immediately with fromage frais or
vanilla ice cream, if you like.

COOK'S TIP
For an accompaniment that won't add
too much to the fat content of this
dessert, make your own frozen yogurt
by churning a low-fat yogurt in an
ice-cream maker.

NUTRITIONAL NOTES
Per portion:

Energy	263Kcals/1110kJ
Fat, total	4.1g
Saturated fat	0.51g
Cholesterol	0.2mg
Fibre	1.6g

CARIBBEAN BANANAS

Tender baked bananas in a rich and spicy sauce of ground allspice and ginger –
the perfect dessert for those with a sweet tooth!

INGREDIENTS
30ml/2 tbsp low-fat spread
8 firm ripe bananas
juice of 1 lime
75g/3oz/1/2 cup soft dark brown sugar
5ml/1 tsp ground allspice
2.5ml/1/2 tsp ground ginger
seeds from 6 cardamoms crushed
30ml/2 tbsp rum
pared lime rind, to decorate
low-fat crème fraîche, to serve (optional)

SERVES 4

1 Preheat the oven to 200°C/400°F/Gas 6.

2 Use a little of the spread to grease a shallow baking dish large enough to hold the bananas snugly in a single layer.

3 Peel the bananas, cut them in half lengthways and arrange them in the dish. Pour over the lime juice.

4 Mix the sugar, allspice, ginger and crushed cardamom seeds in a bowl. Scatter the mixture over the bananas.

5 Dot with the remaining low-fat spread. Bake, basting once, for 15 minutes, or until the bananas are soft.

6 Warm the rum in a small pan or metal soup ladle, pour it over the bananas and set it alight.

7 As soon as the flames die down, decorate the dessert with the pared lime rind.

8 Serve while still hot and add a dollop of crème fraîche to each portion, if you like.

VARIATION
For a version that will appeal more to children, use orange juice instead of lime and leave out the rum.

NUTRITIONAL NOTES
Per portion:

Energy	310Kcals/1306kJ
Fat, total	3.2g
Saturated fat	0.87g
Cholesterol	0.4mg
Fibre	2.2g

SPICED NECTARINES WITH FROMAGE FRAIS

This easy dessert is good at any time of year – use canned peach halves if fresh
nectarines are not available. The riper the fruit, the better the taste of this dessert.

2 Arrange the fruit, cut-side upwards,
in a wide flameproof dish or on a
baking sheet.

3 Stir the sugar into the fromage frais.
Using a teaspoon, spoon the mixture into
the hollow of each half.

4 Sprinkle the fruit with the ground
star anise.

5 Place under a moderately hot grill
(broiler) for 6–8 minutes, or until the fruit
is hot and bubbling. Serve warm.

INGREDIENTS
4 ripe nectarines or peaches
15ml/1 tbsp light muscovado
(brown) sugar
115g/4oz/¹/2 cup low-fat fromage frais
2.5ml/¹/2 tsp ground star anise

SERVES 4

NUTRITIONAL NOTES
Per portion:

Energy	108Kcals/450kJ
Fat, total	3.3g
Saturated fat	2g
Cholesterol	14.4mg
Fibre	1.5g

1 With a sharp knife cut the nectarines
or peaches in half and remove the stones.

COOK'S TIP
If star anise is not available, try ground
cloves or mixed (apple pie) spice.

NECTARINES WITH MARZIPAN AND YOGURT

A luscious dessert that few can resist; the ground almond taste of the marzipan combined with soft and flavourful nectarines are a wonderful combination.

INGREDIENTS
4 firm, ripe nectarines or peaches
75g/3oz marzipan
75ml/5 tbsp low-fat Greek (US strained plain) yogurt
3 amaretti, crushed

SERVES 4

3 Spoon the Greek yogurt on top. Sprinkle the crushed amaretti over the yogurt.

4 Place the fruits on a hot barbecue or under a hot grill (broiler). Cook for 3–5 minutes, until the yogurt starts to melt.

NUTRITIONAL NOTES
Per portion:

Energy	176Kcals/737kJ
Fat, total	4.3g
Saturated fat	0.98g
Cholesterol	3.2mg
Fibre	2.3g

1 Cut the nectarines or peaches in half. Twist gently to open. Remove the stones.

2 Cut the marzipan into eight pieces and press one piece into the stone cavity of each nectarine half. Preheat the grill, unless you are cooking on the barbecue.

COOK'S TIP
Peaches or nectarines can be used for this recipe. If the stone does not pull out easily when you halve the fruit, use a small, sharp knife to cut around it.

APPLES AND RASPBERRIES IN ROSE SYRUP

Inspiration for this dessert stems from the fact that the apple and the raspberry belong to the rose family. The subtle flavours are shared here in an infusion of rose-scented tea.

INGREDIENTS

5ml/1 tsp rose pouchong tea
900ml/1½ pints/3¾ cups boiling water
5ml/1 tsp rose-water (optional)
50g/2oz/¼ cup sugar
5ml/1 tsp lemon juice
5 eating apples
175g/6oz/1½ cups fresh raspberries

SERVES 4

1 Warm a large tea pot. Add the rose pouchong tea, then pour on the boiling water, together with the rose-water, if using. Allow to stand and infuse for 4 minutes.

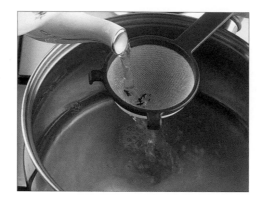

2 Measure the sugar and lemon juice into a stainless steel saucepan. Strain in the tea and stir to dissolve the sugar.

3 Peel and core the apples, then cut into quarters.

4 Poach the apples in the syrup for about 5 minutes.

5 Transfer the apples and syrup to a large baking tray and leave to cool to room temperature.

6 Pour the cooled apples and syrup into a bowl, add the raspberries and mix to combine.

7 Spoon the fruit into individual dishes or bowls and serve at room temperature.

NUTRITIONAL NOTES
Per portion:

Energy	125Kcals/526kJ
Fat, total	0.4g
Saturated fat	0g
Cholesterol	0mg
Fibre	3.6g

PAPAYA BAKED WITH GINGER

Hot ginger enhances the mild flavour of papaya in the sweet, crunchy and tasty topping. This
recipe takes no more than ten minutes to prepare.

INGREDIENTS

2 ripe papayas
8 dessert biscuits, such as ratafias,
coarsely crushed
2 pieces stem ginger in syrup, drained,
plus 15ml/1 tbsp syrup from the jar
45ml/3 tbsp raisins
shredded, finely pared rind and
juice of 1 lime
15ml/1 tbsp light muscovado
(brown) sugar
60ml/4 tbsp low-fat Greek (US strained
plain) yogurt, plus extra
to serve (optional)
15ml/1 tbsp unsalted pistachio nuts,
finely chopped

SERVES 4

1 Preheat the oven to 200°C/400°F/Gas 6.

2 Cut the papayas in half and scoop out
and discard the seeds. Place the fruit in a
baking dish and set aside.

3 Cut the stem ginger into matchsticks
using a sharp knife.

4 To make the filling, combine the
crushed biscuits, stem ginger and raisins
in a bowl and mix together.

5 Stir in the lime rind and juice, then add
the sugar and the yogurt. Mix well.

6 Fill the papaya halves with filling and
drizzle with the ginger syrup. Sprinkle the
pistachios on top.

7 Bake for about 25 minutes or until
tender. Do not overcook. Serve hot, with
extra Greek yogurt, if you like.

NUTRITIONAL NOTES
Per portion:

Energy	218Kcals/922kJ
Fat, total	4.2g
Saturated fat	1.23g
Cholesterol	6mg
Fibre	3.8g

BAKED PEACHES WITH RASPBERRY SAUCE

—

This light dessert is the perfect finale to a dinner party, with its contrasting almond and peach
flavours offset by a tart and flavourful raspberry sauce.

INGREDIENTS

30ml/2 tbsp low-fat spread
50g/2oz/1/4 cup sugar
1 egg, beaten
20g/3/4oz/1/4 cup ground almonds
6 ripe peaches
glossy leaves and plain or frosted
raspberries, to decorate

FOR THE SAUCE

225g/8oz/2 cups raspberries
15ml/1 tbsp icing (confectioners') sugar

SERVES 6

NUTRITIONAL NOTES

Per portion:

Energy	137Kcals/576kJ
Fat, total	4.7g
Saturated fat	0.81g
Cholesterol	32.3mg
Fibre	2.8g

1 Preheat the oven to 180°C/350°F/
Gas 4.

2 In a bowl, beat the low-fat spread and
sugar together, then beat in the egg and
ground almonds.

3 Cut the peaches in half and remove the
stones. With a spoon, scrape out some of
the flesh from each peach half, slightly
enlarging the hollow left by the stone.
Save the excess peach for the sauce.

4 Stand the peach halves on a baking
sheet, supporting them with crumpled foil
to keep them steady. Fill the hollow in
each peach half with the almond mixture.

5 Bake for 30 minutes, or until the
almond filling is puffed and golden and
the peaches are very tender.

6 To make the sauce, combine the
raspberries and icing sugar in a food
processor with the reserved peach flesh.
Process until smooth. Press through a
seive (strainer) set over a bowl to remove
fibres and seeds. Let cool slightly.

7 Spoon the sauce on each plate and
arrange two peach halves on top. Decorate
with the leaves and raspberries.

COOK'S TIP

For a special occasion, stir 15ml/1 tbsp
framboise or peach brandy into the
raspberry sauce.

STUFFED PEACHES WITH ALMOND LIQUEUR

Together amaretti and amaretto have an intense almond flavour, and make a natural partner for peaches. A serving of ice cream adds the finishing touch.

INGREDIENTS

4 ripe, but firm, peaches
50g/2oz/1/2 cup amaretti
30ml/2 tbsp low-fat spread
30ml/2 tbsp caster (superfine) sugar
1 egg yolk
60ml/4 tbsp almond liqueur
low-fat spread, for greasing
250ml/8fl oz/1 cup dry white wine
8 tiny sprigs of fresh basil, to decorate
low-fat ice cream, to serve (optional)

SERVES 4

1 Preheat the oven to 180°C/350°F/Gas 4.

2 Cut the peaches in half and remove the stones. With a spoon, scrape out some of the flesh from each peach half, slightly enlarging the hollow left by the stone. Chop this flesh and set it aside.

3 Put the amaretti in a bowl and crush them with the end of a rolling pin.

4 Cream the low-fat spread and sugar together in a separate bowl until smooth. Stir in the reserved chopped peach flesh, the egg yolk and half the liqueur with the amaretti crumbs. Lightly grease a baking dish that is just large enough to hold the peach halves in a single layer.

NUTRITIONAL NOTES

Per portion:

Energy	232Kcals/971kJ
Fat, total	5g
Saturated fat	1.37g
Cholesterol	54.7mg
Fibre	1.9g

5 Stand the peaches in the dish and spoon the stuffing into them. Mix the remaining liqueur with the wine, pour over the peaches and bake for 25 minutes or until the peaches feel tender. Decorate with basil and serve at once, with low-fat ice cream, if you like.

BARBECUED PINEAPPLE BOATS WITH RUM GLAZE

Fresh pineapple is even more full of flavour when barbecued or grilled (broiled); this spiced rum
glaze turns it into a very special dessert.

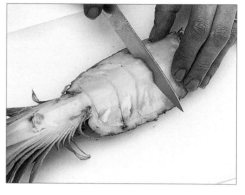

2 Cut between the flesh and skin, to release the flesh, but leave the skin in place. Slice the flesh across, into chunks.

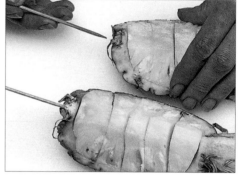

3 Push a bamboo skewer through each wedge and into the stalk, to hold the chunks in place.

4 Mix together the sugar, ginger, melted spread and rum and brush over the pineapple. Cook the wedges on a hot barbecue for 3–4 minutes; pour the remaining glaze over the top and serve.

INGREDIENTS

1 medium pineapple, about 600g/1lb 6oz
30ml/2 tbsp dark muscovado
(molasses) sugar
5ml/1 tsp ground ginger
45ml/3 tbsp low-fat spread, melted
30ml/2 tbsp dark rum

SERVES 4

COOK'S TIP

Use pinepple rings if you like, and
bake in the same way.

1 With a large, sharp knife, cut the pineapple lengthways into four equal wedges. Cut out and discard the hard centre core from each wedge.

NUTRITIONAL NOTES

Per portion:

Energy	155Kcals/646kJ
Fat, total	4.9g
Saturated fat	1.14g
Cholesterol	0.7mg
Fibre	1.8g

PINEAPPLE FLAMBÉ

**Flambéing means adding alcohol and then burning it off so the flavour is not too overpowering.
This dessert is just as good, however, without the brandy or vodka.**

INGREDIENTS

1 large, ripe pineapple, about 600g/1lb 6oz
30ml/2 tbsp low-fat spread
40g/1¹/2 oz/¹/4 cup soft light brown sugar
60ml/4 tbsp fresh orange juice
30ml/2 tbsp brandy or vodka
15g/¹/2 oz/1 tbsp flaked (slivered)
almonds, toasted

SERVES 4

1 Cut off the pineapple top and base. Cut down the sides, removing all the dark 'eyes'. Cut the pineapple into thin slices.

2 Using an apple corer, remove the hard, central core from each slice.

VARIATION
Try this with nectarines, peaches or cherries. Omit the almonds if you want to reduce the fat content a little.

3 Melt the spread in a frying pan, with the sugar. Add the orange juice. Stir until hot.

4 Add as many pineapple slices as the pan will hold and cook for 1–2 minutes, turning once. As each pineapple slice browns, remove it to a plate.

5 Return all the pineapple slices to the pan, heat briefly, then pour over the brandy or vodka and light with a long-handled match. Let the flames die down, then sprinkle with the almonds. Serve at once.

NUTRITIONAL NOTES
Per portion:

Energy	171Kcals/711kJ
Fat, total	5g
Saturated fat	0.62g
Cholesterol	0.4mg
Fibre	2.1g

COOL FRUIT
PUDDINGS AND
DESSERTS

Warmer days call for light desserts and this chapter has a delightful selection of recipes to try that are
big on taste, and sweet enough to satisfy any sugar cravings, while still being low in fat. These delicious
puddings will help you keep on track, adding sweet flavours while going easy on the calories. Tropical fruits are
perfect for desserts and are available all year around. A Two-tone Yogurt Ring with Tropical Fruit is just the
thing for dinner with friends, while Summer Pudding, made with seasonal summer berries, is a time-honoured
favourite that will go down well with anyone. Figs with Ricotta Cream make the most of
in-season fruit, and Greek Fig and Honey Pudding is perfect for any time.

RICH BLACKCURRANT COULIS

There can be few more impressive desserts than this – port wine jelly with swirled cream hearts.
The success of this dessert lies in the intensity of the flavour of the fruit.

INGREDIENTS
6 sheets of leaf gelatine
475ml/16fl oz/2 cups water
450g/1lb blackcurrants
225g/8oz/1 cup caster (superfine) sugar
150ml/¼ pint/²⁄₃ cup ruby port
30ml/2 tbsp crème de cassis or
blackcurrant liqueur
120ml/4fl oz/½ cup single (light) cream,
to decorate

SERVES 8

1 In a small bowl, soak the gelatine in 75ml/5 tbsp of the water until soft.

2 Place the blackcurrants, sugar and 300ml/½ pint/1¼ cups of the remaining water in a large pan. Bring to the boil, lower the heat and simmer for 20 minutes.

3 Strain, reserving the cooking liquid in a large jug (pitcher).

4 Put half the blackcurrants in a bowl and pour over 60ml/4 tbsp of the reserved cooking liquid. (Freeze the remaining blackcurrants to serve as a sauce with ice cream on another day.) Set aside.

5 Squeeze the water out of the gelatine and place in a small pan with the port, cassis and remaining water. Heat gently to dissolve the gelatine but do not allow the mixture to boil.

6 Stir the gelatine mixture into the jug of blackcurrant liquid until well mixed.

7 Place 6–8 jelly moulds in a roasting tin. Fill with the port mixture. Chill for at least 6 hours until set.

8 Purée the blackcurrants in a food processor until smooth, then sieve the purée. Taste and adjust the sweetness.

9 Unmould each jelly on to a serving plate and spoon the coulis around. To decorate, drop a little cream at intervals on to the coulis. Draw a cocktail stick through the cream, dragging each in into a heart shape.

NUTRITIONAL NOTES
Per portion:

Energy	276Kcals/1163kJ
Fat, total	3.8g
Saturated fat	2.4g
Cholesterol	11mg
Fibre	2.7g

SUMMER PUDDING

Summer pudding is an annual treat that is naturally low in fat. Serve it with low fat natural yogurt, Greek yogurt or low-fat ice cream for a filling fruity dessert.

3 Tip the redcurrant mixture into a food processor and process until quite smooth. Press through a fine-mesh nylon strainer set in a bowl. Discard the fruit pulp left in the strainer.

4 Put the mixed berries in a bowl with the remaining sugar and the lemon juice. Stir well.

5 One at a time, remove the cut bread pieces from the basin and dip them in the redcurrant purée. Replace to line the basin evenly.

6 Spoon the berries into the lined basin, pressing them down evenly. Top with the reserved cut bread slices, which have been dipped in the redcurrant purée.

7 Cover the basin with clear film. Set a small plate, just big enough to fit inside the rim of the basin, on top of the pudding. Weigh it down with cans of food. Chill in the refrigerator for 8–24 hours.

8 To turn out, remove the weights, plate and clear film. Run a knife between the basin and the pudding to loosen it. Invert on to a serving plate.

9 Decorate with a sprig of mint and a few berries. Serve in wedges.

INGREDIENTS

1 loaf of white crusty bread,
1–2 days old, sliced, crusts removed
675g/1 1/2 lb/6 cups fresh redcurrants
75g/3oz/6 tbsp sugar
60ml/4 tbsp water
450g/1lb/4 cups mixed berries, plus extra
to decorate
sprig of mint, to decorate
juice of 1/2 lemon

SERVES 6

NUTRITIONAL NOTES
Per portion:

Energy	272Kcals/1152kJ
Fat, total	1.6g
Saturated fat	0g
Cholesterol	0mg
Fibre	7.6g

1 Cut a round of bread to fit in the base of a 1.5 litre/2 1/2 pint/6-cup pudding basin. Line the basin with bread slices, overlapping them slightly. Reserve enough bread slices to cover the top of the basin.

2 Mix the redcurrants with 50g/2oz/ 1/4 cup of the sugar and the water in a pan. Heat gently, crushing the berries lightly to help the juices flow. When the sugar has dissolved, remove from the heat.

STRAWBERRIES IN SPICED GRAPE JELLY

The spicy cinnamon combines with the sun-ripened strawberries to make a delectable
and very low-fat dessert for a summer dinner party.

INGREDIENTS

475ml/16fl oz/2 cups red grape juice
1 cinnamon stick
1 small orange, thinly pared
15ml/1 tbsp powdered gelatine
225g/8oz/2 cups strawberries, chopped,
plus extra to decorate

SERVES 4

1 Pour the grape juice into a pan, add
the cinnamon stick and the pared
orange rind.

2 Place the pan over a very low heat for
10 minutes, then remove the flavourings
from the grape juice.

3 Squeeze the juice from the orange into
a bowl and sprinkle over the gelatine.
When the mixture is spongy, stir into the
grape juice until it dissolves.

4 Allow the jelly to cool in the bowl until
just beginning to set.

5 Stir in the strawberries and quickly tip
into a 1 litre/1¾ pint/4 cup mould or
serving dish. Chill until set.

6 Dip the mould quickly into hot water
and invert on to a serving plate. Decorate
with strawberries and shreds of orange rind.

NUTRITIONAL NOTES
Per portion:

Energy	85Kcals/355kJ
Fat, total	0.2g
Saturated fat	0g
Cholesterol	0mg
Fibre	1.04g

ORANGE-BLOSSOM JELLY

—

A fresh orange jelly makes a delightful dessert; the natural fruit flavour combined with the smooth jelly has a wonderful cleansing quality.

INGREDIENTS

65g/2¹/₂ oz/5 tbsp caster (superfine) sugar
150ml/¹/₄ pint/²/₃ cup water
25g/1oz powdered gelatine
600ml/1 pint/2¹/₂ cups fresh orange juice
30ml/2 tbsp orange-flower water

SERVES 4

1 Put the sugar and water in a pan and heat gently to dissolve the sugar. Pour into a heatproof bowl and leave to cool.

2 Sprinkle the gelatine over the syrup. Leave the gelatine to absorb the liquid.

NUTRITIONAL NOTES

Per portion:

Energy	135Kcals/573kJ
Fat, total	0g
Saturated fat	0g
Cholesterol	0mg
Fibre	0.2g

3 Melt the gelatine over a pan of gently simmering water until it turns clear. Leave to go cold, then pour the orange juice and orange-flower water into it.

4 Pour the jelly into a mould. Refrigerate for at least 2 hours, or until set.

5 Place the jelly mould in warm water for a few seconds, then unmould on to a plate.

COOK'S TIP

Substitute Grand Marnier for the orange-flower water.

RICE FRUIT SUNDAE

Cook a rice pudding on top of the stove instead of in the oven for a light creamy texture,
which is particularly good served cold topped with fruits.

NUTRITIONAL NOTES
Per portion:

Energy	169Kcals/711kJ
Fat, total	3.3g
Saturated fat	0.1g
Cholesterol	3mg
Fibre	0.9g

2 Allow the rice to cool, stirring occasionally. When cold, refrigerate until ready to serve.

3 Just before serving, stir the rice and spoon into four sundae dishes. Top with the prepared fruit.

INGREDIENTS
*50g/2oz/¹/3 cup short-grain
(pudding) rice
600ml/1 pint/2¹/2 cups skimmed
(very low-fat) milk
5ml/1 tsp vanilla extract
2.5ml/¹/2 tsp ground cinnamon
25g/1oz/2 tbsp sugar
200g/7oz/1³/4 cups strawberries,
raspberries or blueberries, to serve*

SERVES 4

1 Put the rice, milk, vanilla, cinnamon and sugar into a pan. Bring to the boil, stirring constantly. Turn down the heat and simmer for 30–40 minutes, stirring.

VARIATION
Instead of simple pudding rice try using a Thai fragrant or jasmine rice for a delicious natural flavour. For a firmer texture, an Italian arborio rice makes a good pudding too. You could also use other toppings, such as toasted, chopped hazelnuts or toasted coconut flakes. Other fruit combinations could be mango, pineapple and banana for a tropical taste. Sweet fruit complements the pudding rice best.

SENSATIONAL STRAWBERRIES

—

Buy large juicy strawberries at the height of the season for this recipe. With so few ingredients, all need to be at their flavourful best.

INGREDIENTS
350g/12oz/3 cups raspberries, fresh or frozen
45ml/3 tbsp caster (superfine) sugar
1 passion fruit
675g/1½ lb small strawberries
sponge fingers, to serve (optional)

SERVES 4

1 Mix the raspberries and sugar in a pan and heat gently until the raspberries release their juices. Simmer for 5 minutes. Leave to cool.

2 Cut the passion fruit in half and scoop out the seeds and juice into a bowl.

3 Tip the raspberry mixture into a food processor or blender, add the passion fruit and blend to a smooth purée.

4 Press the purée through a fine sieve placed over a bowl, to remove the seeds.

5 Fold the strawberries into the sauce, then spoon into four stemmed glasses. Serve with sponge fingers or any sweet dessert biscuits, and serve at room temperature for best results.

COOK'S TIP
This recipe can be made ahead of eating and chilled. Remove from the refrigerator half an hour before serving.

NUTRITIONAL NOTES
Per portion:

Energy	115Kcals/484kJ
Fat, total	0.5g
Saturated fat	0g
Cholesterol	0mg
Fibre	4.2g

TWO-TONE YOGURT RING WITH TROPICAL FRUIT

—

**An impressive, light and colourful dessert with a truly tropical flavour,
combining the flavours of mango, kiwi fruit and physalis.**

INGREDIENTS

175ml/6fl oz/³/4 cup tropical fruit juice
15ml/1 tbsp powdered gelatine
3 egg whites
*150ml/¹/4 pint/²/3 cup low-fat
natural (plain) yogurt*
finely grated rind of 1 lime

FOR THE FILLING

1 mango
2 kiwi fruit
*10–12 physalis (Cape gooseberries),
plus extra to decorate*
juice of 1 lime

SERVES 6

1 Pour the tropical fruit juice into a small pan and sprinkle the powdered gelatine over the surface. Heat gently until the gelatine has dissolved.

2 Whisk the egg whites in a grease-free bowl until they hold soft peaks. Continue whisking hard, gradually adding the yogurt and lime rind.

3 Continue whisking hard and pour in the hot gelatine mixture in a steady stream, until evenly mixed.

4 Quickly pour the mixture into a 1.5 litre/2¹/2 pint/6¹/4 cup ring mould. Chill in the refrigerator until set. The mixture will separate into two layers.

5 Prepare the filling. Halve, stone (pit), peel and dice the mango. Peel and slice the kiwi fruit. Remove the husks from the physalis and cut them in half. Toss all the fruits together in a bowl and stir in the lime juice.

6 Run a knife around the edge of the ring to loosen the mixture. Dip the tin quickly into hot water, then turn it out on to a serving plate. Spoon all the prepared fruit into the centre of the ring, decorate with the reserved physalis and serve immediately.

NUTRITIONAL NOTES
Per portion:

Energy	87Kcals/364kJ
Fat, total	0.5g
Saturated fat	0.13g
Cholesterol	1mg
Fibre	2.3g

VARIATION
Any mixture of fruit works in
this recipe, depending on the season.
Try using apple juice in the ring
mixture and fill it with luscious,
red summer fruits.

PASSION FRUIT AND APPLE FOAM

Passion fruit have an exotic, scented flavour that really lifts this simple apple dessert.
If passion fruit are not available, use two finely chopped kiwi fruit instead.

INGREDIENTS
450g/1lb cooking apples
90ml/6 tbsp unsweetened apple juice
3 passion fruit
3 egg whites
1 red-skinned eating apple, to decorate
5ml/1 tsp lemon juice

SERVES 4

1 Peel, core and roughly chop the cooking apples. Put them in a pan with the apple juice.

2 Bring to the boil, then lower the heat and cover the pan. Cook gently, stirring occasionally, until the apple is tender.

COOK'S TIP
You can use dessert apples for this recipe, but will probably have to purée them in a food processor.

3 Remove from the heat and beat the apple mixture with a wooden spoon until it forms a fairly smooth purée (or purée the apple in a food processor if you prefer).

4 Cut the passion fruit in half and scoop out the flesh. Stir the flesh into the apple purée to mix thoroughly.

5 Place the egg whites in a grease-free bowl and whisk them until they form soft peaks.

6 Fold the egg whites into the apple mixture. Spoon the apple foam into four serving dishes. Leave to cool.

7 Thinly slice the red-skinned apple and brush the slices with lemon juice to prevent them from browning.

8 Arrange the slices on top of the apple foam and serve cold.

NUTRITIONAL NOTES
Per portion:

Energy	80Kcals/338kJ
Fat, total	0.2g
Saturated fat	0g
Cholesterol	0mg
Fibre	2.9g

RASPBERRY AND MINT BAVAROIS

—

A sophisticated and smooth dessert, made with minimal ingredients, that can be made a day in advance for a special dinner party.

INGREDIENTS

450g/1lb/4 cups fresh or
thawed frozen raspberries
30ml/2 tbsp icing (confectioners') sugar
30ml/2 tbsp lemon juice
15ml/1 tbsp finely chopped fresh mint
30ml/2 tbsp powdered gelatine
75ml/5 tbsp boiling water
300ml/1/2 pint/1¼ cups low-fat custard
250ml/8fl oz/1 cup low-fat Greek
(US strained plain) yogurt
fresh mint sprigs, to decorate

SERVES 6

1 Reserve a few raspberries for the decoration. Place the remaining raspberries in a food processor.

2 Add the icing sugar and lemon juice and process the raspberries to a smooth purée.

NUTRITIONAL NOTES
Per portion:

Energy	131Kcals/554kJ
Fat, total	2.4g
Saturated fat	1.36g
Cholesterol	4.1mg
Fibre	1.9g

3 Press the purée through a sieve to remove the raspberry seeds. Pour it into a measuring jug and stir in the mint.

4 Sprinkle 5ml/1 tsp of the gelatine over 30ml/2 tbsp of the boiling water and stir until the gelatine has dissolved. Stir into 150ml/1/4 pint/2/3 cup of the fruit purée.

5 Pour this jelly into a 1 litre/1¾ pint/ 4 cup mould, and refrigerate until the jelly is just setting. Tip the tin to swirl the setting jelly around the sides, and leave to chill until the jelly has set completely.

6 Mix the custard and low-fat Greek yogurt in a bowl and stir in the remaining fruit purée.

7 Dissolve the rest of the gelatine in the remaining boiling water and stir it in quickly.

8 Pour the raspberry custard into the mould and chill it until it has set completely. To serve, dip the mould quickly into hot water and then turn it out on a serving plate. Decorate with the reserved raspberries and the mint sprigs.

COOK'S TIP
You can make this dessert using frozen raspberries, which have a good colour and flavour. Allow them to thaw at room temperature, and use any juice in the jelly.

BRAZILIAN COFFEE BANANAS

Rich, lavish and sinful-looking, this low-fat dessert takes only about
two minutes to make and marginally longer to eat. Delicious!

INGREDIENTS

4 small ripe bananas, peeled
15ml/1 tbsp instant coffee granules
or powder
15ml/1 tbsp hot water
30ml/2 tbsp dark muscovado
(molasses) sugar
250ml/8fl oz/1 cup low-fat Greek
(US strained plain) yogurt
10ml/2 tsp flaked (slivered)
almonds, toasted

SERVES 4

NUTRITIONAL NOTES
Per portion:

Energy	175Kcals/736kJ
Fat, total	4.8g
Saturated fat	2.06g
Cholesterol	4.4mg
Fibre	1.1g

3 Spoon a little of the mashed banana mixture into four serving dishes and sprinkle each with sugar. Top with a spoonful of yogurt, then repeat the layers until all the ingredients are used up.

4 Swirl the last layer of yogurt for a marbled effect.

5 Add a few banana and almonds. Serve cold. Eat within an hour of making.

1 Slice one banana and mash the rest.

2 Dissolve the coffee in the hot water and stir into the mashed bananas.

VARIATION
Add 15ml/1 tbsp of rum or brandy to the dessert, and add 30 calories.

RASPBERRIES AND FRUIT PURÉE

Three fruit purées, swirled together, make a kaleidoscopic garnish for a nest of raspberries.
It also makes a perfect accommpaniement to meringue and ice cream.

INGREDIENTS
200g/7oz raspberries
120ml/4fl oz/¹/2 cup red wine
icing (confectioners') sugar, to sweeten

FOR THE DECORATION
1 large mango, peeled and chopped
400g/14oz kiwi fruit, peeled and chopped
200g/7oz raspberries
icing (confectioners') sugar, for dusting

SERVES 4–6

1 Place the raspberries in a bowl with the red wine and allow to macerate for about 2 hours.

2 To make the decoration, purée the mango in a food processor, adding water if necessary. Press through a sieve.

3 Purée the kiwi fruit in the same way, then make a third purée from the remaining raspberries. Sweeten, if necessary.

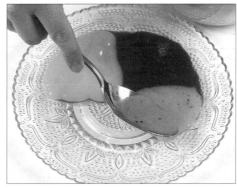

4 Spoon each purée on to a serving plate, separating the kiwi and mango with the raspberry purée as if creating a four-wedged pie. Gently tap the plate on the work surface to settle the purées against each other.

5 Using a skewer, draw a spiral outwards from the centre of the plate to the rim. Drain the macerated raspberries, pile them in the centre, and dust them heavily with icing sugar.

NUTRITIONAL NOTES
Per portion:

Energy	154Kcals/648kJ
Fat, total	0.9g
Saturated fat	0g
Cholesterol	0mg
Fibre	6.7g

GREEK FIG AND HONEY PUDDING

—

A quick pudding that is light and easy to eat as well as make, made from fresh figs topped with
yogurt, drizzled with honey and sprinkled with pistachio nuts.

2 Stir the Greek yogurt and natural yogurt together.

3 Top each glass or bowl of figs with a quarter of the mixture. Chill until ready to serve.

4 Just before serving drizzle 15ml/1 tbsp honey over each dessert and sprinkle with the pistachio nuts.

INGREDIENTS
4 fresh figs
*250ml/8fl oz/1 cup low-fat Greek
(US strained plain) yogurt*
*250ml/8fl oz/1 cup low-fat natural
(plain) yogurt*
60ml/4 tbsp clear honey
*10ml/2 tsp chopped, unsalted
pistachio nuts*

SERVES 4

1 Chop the figs and place in the base of four stemmed glasses or deep, individual dessert bowls.

NUTRITIONAL NOTES
Per portion:

Energy	158Kcals/664kJ
Fat, total	4.7g
Saturated fat	2.21g
Cholesterol	6.1mg
Fibre	0.8g

FIGS WITH RICOTTA CREAM

Fresh, ripe figs are full of natural sweetness. This simple recipe makes the most of their
beautiful, intense flavour. Buy them when they are in their natural season for best flavour.

INGREDIENTS
4 ripe, fresh figs
115g/4oz/1/2 cup ricotta cheese
45ml/3 tbsp half-fat crème fraîche
15ml/1 tbsp clear honey
2.5ml/1/2 tsp pure vanilla extract
freshly grated nutmeg, to decorate

SERVES 4

COOK'S TIP
The honey can be omitted and replaced
with a little artificial sweetener.

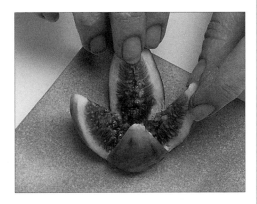

1 Using a small sharp knife, trim the
stalks from the figs. Make four cuts
through each fig from the stalk-end,
cutting them almost through but being
careful to leave them joined at the base.

2 Place the figs on serving plates and
open them out. Very ripe fruits will be
very soft so take care.

3 In a bowl, mix together the ricotta
cheese, crème fraîche, honey and
vanilla extract. Taste and add more honey
or vanilla if necessary.

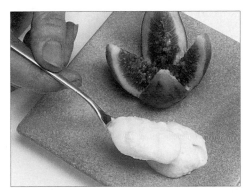

4 Spoon a little ricotta cream mixture on
to each plate and sprinkle with grated
nutmeg to serve.

NUTRITIONAL NOTES
Per portion:

Energy	97Kcals/405kJ
Fat, total	5.0g
Saturated fat	3.04g
Cholesterol	26.2mg
Fibre	0.8g

PASTRIES, PANCAKES AND MERINGUES

Thin as tissue paper, light and crunchy filo pastry is the perfect choice for a sumptuous dessert without breaking the diet rules. Use it to make parcels and baskets and fill them with sweet summer fruit, bake them and serve with low-fat Greek yogurt. Meringues and pancakes too are light and airy desserts that can also be filled with winning combinations of summer berries, poached to make compote and topped with low-fat ice cream to add richness. Use whatever fruit is in season for quick and easy dessert treats. Pastries and pancakes are best baked and eaten fresh for best taste. Meringues will store for later use, when a quick-to-make dessert is needed in an instant.

FILO RHUBARB CHIFFON PIE

Filo pastry is low in fat and is very easy to bake. Keep a pack in the freezer, ready to make impressive puddings like this one, but remember to add defrosting time into your recipe plan.

INGREDIENTS
500g/1¼ lb pink rhubarb
5ml/1 tsp mixed (apple pie) spice
finely grated rind and juice of 1 orange
15ml/1 tbsp sugar
15ml/1 tbsp low-fat spread
3 sheets filo pastry, thawed if frozen

SERVES 3

VARIATION
Other fruit such as apples, pears or peaches can be used in this pie – try it with whatever is in season.

---

1 Preheat the oven to 200°C/400°F/ Gas 6.

2 Trim the leaves and ends from the rhubarb sticks and chop them in to 2.5cm/1in pieces. Place them in a mixing bowl.

3 Add the mixed spice, orange rind and juice and sugar; toss well to coat evenly. Tip the rhubarb into a 1 litre/1¾ pint/ 4-cup pie dish.

4 Melt the spread and brush over the filo sheets. Crumple the filo loosely and place the pieces on top of the filling to cover.

5 Place the dish on a baking sheet and bake the pie for 20 minutes, until golden brown. Reduce the heat to 180°C/350°F/ Gas 4 and bake for 10–15 minutes more until the rhubarb is tender. Serve warm.

NUTRITIONAL NOTES
Per portion:

Energy	118Kcals/494kJ
Fat, total	3g
Saturated fat	0.65g
Cholesterol	0.3mg
Fibre	2.4g

SPICED MANGO FILO FINGERS

Filo pastry, butter, sugar and tropical fruit are the basic ingredients for a light and flavourful
dessert made in heaven, which is perfect to serve for any occasion.

INGREDIENTS
4 mangoes
6 filo pastry sheets
90g/3¹/₂oz/7 tbsp low-fat spread, melted
45g/3 tbsp soft light brown sugar
20ml/4 tsp ground cinnamon
icing (confectioners') sugar, for dusting

SERVES 8

1 Preheat the oven to 200°C/400°F/Gas 6.

2 Set one mango aside for decoration.
Peel the remaining mangoes. Slice the
flesh into 3mm/¹/₈in thick slices.

3 Place one sheet of filo on a baking
sheet and brush with melted spread. Mix
the brown sugar and cinnamon together
and sprinkle one-fifth of the mixture over
the filo. Place another sheet of filo on top
and repeat for the other 5 sheets, ending
with a filo sheet.

NUTRITIONAL NOTES
Per portion:

Energy	207Kcals/861kJ
Fat, total	5.0g
Saturated fat	2.75g
Cholesterol	11.5mg
Fibre	3.6g

4 Brush the top filo sheet with butter,
trim off the excess pastry and arrange the
sliced mango in neat rows across the
layered filo, to cover it completely.
Brush with reserved butter and bake for
30 minutes. Allow to cool on the baking
tray, then cut into fingers.

5 Slice the flesh from each side of the
stone of the reserved mango. Cut each
piece in half lengthways. Make four long
cuts, almost to the end, in each quarter.
Dust with icing sugar. Put on a plate and
carefully fan out the slices. Serve with the
mango fingers.

APRICOT PARCELS

These little filo parcels contain a special apricot and mincemeat filling. A good way to use up any
mincemeat and marzipan that have been in your cupboard since Christmas!

NUTRITIONAL NOTES
Per portion:

Energy	234Kcals/982kJ
Fat, total	4.4g
Saturated fat	1.1g
Cholesterol	3.7mg
Fibre	1.5g

3 Place an apricot half, hollow up, on
the work surface. Mix together the
mincemeat, crushed ratafias and
marzipan and spoon a little of the mixture
into the hollow in each apricot. Top with
another apricot half.

4 Place each filled apricot on a pastry
star then bring the corners of each pastry
together and squeeze to make a
gathered purse.

5 Place the purses on a baking sheet and
brush each with a little melted spread.

6 Bake for 15–20 minutes or until the
pastry is golden and crisp. Lightly dust
with icing sugar to serve.

INGREDIENTS
350g/12oz filo pastry, thawed if frozen
30ml/2 tbsp low-fat spread, melted
8 apricots, halved and stoned
60ml/4 tbsp luxury mincemeat
12 ratafias, crushed
30ml/2 tbsp grated marzipan
icing (confectioners') sugar, for dusting

SERVES 8

1 Preheat the oven to 200°C/400°F/Gas 6.

2 Cut the filo into 32 squares each
18cm/7in. Brush four of the squares with
melted spread and stack them, giving
each layer a quarter turn so that the stack
acquires a star shape. Repeat to make
eight stars.

COOK'S TIP
If you have run out of mincemeat,
use mixed vine fruits instead.

FILO FRUIT SCRUNCHIES

—

Quick and easy to make, these pastries are ideal to serve after a light evening meal. Eat them
warm or they will lose their crispness.

INGREDIENTS
5 apricots or plums
4 sheets filo pastry, thawed if frozen
20ml/4 tsp low-fat spread, melted
50g/2oz/1/3 cup demerara (raw) sugar
30ml/2 tbsp flaked (slivered) almonds
icing (confectioners') sugar, for dusting

SERVES 6

1 Preheat the oven to 190°C/375°F/Gas 5.
Halve the apricots or plums, remove the
stones and slice the fruit.

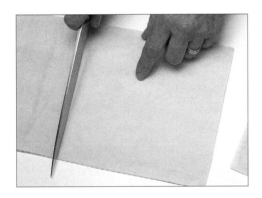

2 Cut the filo pastry into 12 squares each
18cm/7in. Pile the squares on top of each
other and cover with a clean dish towel to
prevent the pastry from drying out.

3 Remove one square of filo and brush it
with melted spread. Place a second filo
square on top, then, using your fingers,
mould the pastry into folds. Make five
more quickly before the pastry dries.

4 Arrange a few slices of fruit in the folds
of each scrunchie.

5 Sprinkle generously with the demerara
sugar and flaked almonds. Place the
scrunchies on a baking sheet.

6 Bake for 8–10 minutes until golden
brown, then loosen the scrunchies from
the baking sheet with a palette knife and
transfer to a wire rack.

7 Dust with icing sugar and serve at once.

NUTRITIONAL NOTES
Per portion:

Energy	132Kcals/555kJ
Fat, total	4.19g
Saturated fat	0.63g
Cholesterol	0mg
Fibre	0.67g

TROPICAL FRUIT FILO CLUSTERS

These fruity filo clusters are ideal for a family treat or a dinner party dessert. They are delicious served either hot or cold, on their own or with reduced-fat cream.

INGREDIENTS

1 banana, sliced
1 small mango, peeled, stoned (pitted)
and diced
lemon juice, for sprinkling
1 small cooking apple, coarsely grated
6 fresh or dried dates, stoned
(pitted) and chopped
50g/2oz/¹/₃ cup ready-to-eat dried
pineapple, chopped
50g/2oz/¹/₃ cup sultanas (golden raisins)
50g/2oz/¹/₃ cup soft light brown sugar
5ml/1 tsp ground mixed spice
8 sheets filo pastry, thawed if frozen
30ml/2 tbsp sunflower oil
icing (confectioners') sugar, for dusting

SERVES 8

NUTRITIONAL NOTES
Per portion:

Energy	197Kcals/833kJ
Fat, total	3.58g
Saturated fat	0.44g
Cholesterol	0mg
Fibre	2.31g

1 Preheat the oven to 200°C/400°F/ Gas 6.

2 Toss the banana and mango in the lemon juice to prevent discoloration.

3 Add the apple, dates, pineapple, sultanas, sugar and spice to the bowl and mix well.

4 To make each fruit cluster, cut each sheet of filo pastry in half (16 pieces in total). Lightly brush two pieces of pastry with oil and place one on top of the other at a 45 degree angle. Work quickly so the pastry does not dry out.

5 Spoon some fruit filling into the centre, gather the pastry up over the filling and secure with string.

6 Line a baking sheet with baking parchment.

7 Place the cluster on the prepared baking sheet and lightly brush all over with oil.

8 Repeat with the remaining pastry squares and filling to make a total of eight fruit clusters.

9 Bake for 25–30 minutes, until golden brown and crisp.

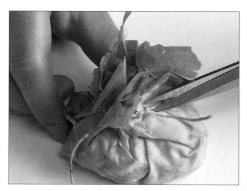

10 Carefully snip and remove the string from each cluster and serve hot or cold, dusted with sifted icing sugar.

COOK'S TIP
To prevent filo pastry drying out and crumbling, cover with a damp cloth before brushing with the oil.

REDCURRANT FILO BASKETS

Filo pastry is crisp and light and makes a very elegant dessert. It is also low in fat and needs only
a fine brushing of oil before use; a light oil such as sunflower is the best choice for this recipe.

INGREDIENTS

3 sheets filo pastry, thawed if frozen
15ml/1 tbsp sunflower oil
175g/6oz/1¹/₂ cups redcurrants
250ml/8fl oz/1 cup low-fat Greek
(US strained plain) yogurt
5ml/1 tsp icing (confectioners') sugar

SERVES 6

1 Preheat the oven to 200°C/400°F/Gas 6.

2 Cut the sheets of filo pastry into 18
squares each 10cm/4in. Brush each filo
square thinly with oil.

3 Arrange three squares in each of six
cupcake tins (pans), placing each at a
different angle to form star-shapes.

4 Bake for 6–8 minutes, until crisp and
golden. Lift the pastries out carefully and
leave them to cool on a wire rack.

5 Set aside a few sprigs of redcurrants on
their stems for decoration and string the
rest. Stir the redcurrants into the low-fat
Greek yogurt.

6 Spoon the yogurt into the filo baskets.
Decorate them with the reserved sprigs of
redcurrants and sprinkle them with the
icing sugar to serve.

NUTRITIONAL NOTES
Per portion:

Energy	80Kcals/335kJ
Fat, total	3.8g
Saturated fat	1.35g
Cholesterol	2.3mg
Fibre	1g

FILO FRUIT BASKETS

Crisp filo teamed with pineapple, raspberries and grapes set in a strawberry yogurt cream
makes a fine finale for a summer meal. Serve with single cream for a special occasion.

INGREDIENTS
4 large or 8 small sheets of filo pastry,
thawed if frozen
25g/1oz/5 tsp low-fat spread, melted
250ml/8fl oz/1 cup low-fat Greek
(US strained plain) yogurt
60ml/4 tbsp strawberry jam
15ml/1 tbsp orange liqueur
115g/4oz/1 cup seedless red grapes, halved
115g/4oz/1 cup seedless green
grapes, halved
175g/6oz/1 cup fresh pineapple cubes
225g/8oz/2 cups raspberries
30ml/2 tbsp icing (confectioners') sugar
6 small sprigs of fresh mint, for decorating

SERVES 6

1 Preheat the oven to 180°C/350°F/Gas 4.
Grease 6 cups of a cupcake tin (pan).

2 Stack the filo sheets and cut into
24 squares each 12cm/4½ in.

NUTRITIONAL NOTES
Per portion:

Energy	207Kcals/867kJ
Fat, total	4.6g
Saturated fat	1.84g
Cholesterol	3.2mg
Fibre	1.4g

3 Arrange four pastry squares in each of
the six tins. Press firmly into the tins,
rotating to make star-shaped baskets.

4 Brush the pastry baskets lightly with
melted low-fat spread. Bake for
5–7 minutes, until the pastry is crisp
and golden. Cool on a wire rack.

5 In a bowl, mix the yogurt with the
strawberry jam and liqueur.

6 Just before serving, spoon a little of the
cream mixture into each pastry basket.

7 Top with the fruit. Sprinkle with icing
sugar and decorate each basket with a
small sprig of mint.

BLUEBERRY PANCAKES

These fairly thick American-style pancakes were made popular as a breakfast option,
but they are equally good as a filling dessert.

3 Heat a few drops of oil in a pancake pan or heavy frying pan until just hazy.

4 Pour on about 30ml/2 tbsp of the batter and swirl it around until it makes a neat pancake.

5 Cook for 2–3 minutes. When almost set on top, sprinkle over 15–30ml/1–2 tbsp of the blueberries. As soon as the base is loose and golden brown, turn the pancake over.

6 Cook on the second side for only about 1 minute, until golden and crisp. Slide the pancake on to a plate and keep warm while you make 17 more pancakes in the same way.

7 Serve drizzled with maple syrup, if you like, and offer lemon wedges for squeezing, if using.

INGREDIENTS
*115g/4oz/1 cup self-raising
(self-rising) flour
pinch of salt
40g/1¹/2 oz/3 tbsp caster (superfine) sugar
2 eggs, beaten
120ml/4fl oz/¹/2 cup skimmed
(very low-fat) milk
15ml/1 tbsp vegetable oil
115g/4oz fresh or frozen blueberries
maple syrup and miniature lemon wedges,
to serve (optional)*

SERVES 6

VARIATION
Instead of blueberries you could use blackberries or raspberries.

1 Sift the flour and salt into a bowl. Add the sugar. Make a well in the middle of the flour and stir in the beaten eggs.

2 Gradually blend in a little of the milk to make a smooth batter. Then whisk in the rest of the milk and continue to whisk for 1–2 minutes. Allow the batter to rest for 20–30 minutes.

NUTRITIONAL NOTES
Per portion:

Energy	146Kcals/618kJ
Fat, total	3.9g
Saturated fat	0.76g
Cholesterol	64.6mg
Fibre	0.9g

TROPICAL FRUIT PANCAKES

Fresh fruit, coated with a citrus and honey sauce, makes the perfect pancake filling
for this light and tasty dessert. Experiment with different fruit combinations for this recipe.

INGREDIENTS

*115g/4oz/1 cup self-raising
(self-rising) flour
pinch of grated nutmeg
15ml/1 tbsp caster (superfine) sugar
1 egg
300ml/¹/₂ pint/1¹/₄ cups skimmed
(very low-fat) milk
15ml/1 tbsp low-fat spread, melted
15ml/1 tbsp fine desiccated (dry
unsweetened shredded) coconut (optional)
light sunflower spray oil, for frying
icing (confectioners') sugar, for dusting
low-fat Greek (US strained plain) yogurt,
to serve (optional)*

FOR THE FILLING

*225g/8oz ripe, firm mango, diced
2 bananas, chopped
2 kiwi fruit, peeled and sliced
1 large orange
15ml/1 tbsp lemon juice
30ml/2 tbsp unsweetened orange juice
15ml/1 tbsp clear honey*

SERVES 4

1 In a bowl, beat the egg, then add most
of the milk. Sift the flour, nutmeg and
sugar over and beat to make a thick,
smooth batter.

2 Add the remaining milk, melted spread
and coconut, if using, and beat until the
batter has a thin, dropping consistency.

3 For the filling, mix the mango with the
bananas and kiwi fruit. Peel the orange
and cut into segments. Place in a bowl.

4 Mix the lemon and orange juices and
honey, then pour over the fruit.

5 Spray a non-stick frying pan with a
very thin coating of oil. Heat, then pour in
a little batter to cover the pan base. Fry
until golden, then turn with a spatula.
Repeat to make eight pancakes.

6 Spoon a little fruit down the centre of a
pancake and fold over each side. Repeat
with the remaining pancakes, then dust
with icing sugar and serve solo or with
low-fat Greek yogurt.

NUTRITIONAL NOTES

Per portion:

Energy	303Kcals/1280kJ
Fat, total	4.7g
Saturated fat	0.98g
Cholesterol	49.9mg
Fibre	4.2g

SUMMER BERRY CRÊPES

—

Lavish and appealing to look at and even better to taste, the delicate flavour of these fluffy
crêpes contrasts beautifully with tangy berry fruits.

INGREDIENTS

115g/4oz/1 cup self-raising
(self-rising) flour
1 large egg
300ml/¹/2 pint/1¹/4 cups skimmed
(very low-fat) milk
1.5ml/¹/4 tsp vanilla extract
spray oil, for greasing
icing (confectioners') sugar, for dusting

FOR THE FRUIT

15ml/1 tbsp low-fat spread
50g/2oz/¹/4 cup caster (superfine) sugar
juice of 2 oranges
thinly pared rind of ¹/2 orange
350g/12oz/3 cups mixed summer berries,
such as sliced strawberries, yellow
raspberries, blueberries and redcurrants
45ml/3 tbsp Grand Marnier or other
orange-flavoured liqueur

SERVES 4

1 Preheat the oven to 150°C/300°F/Gas 2.

2 To make the crêpes, sift the flour into a
large bowl and make a well in the centre.

3 Break in the egg and gradually whisk
in the milk to make a smooth batter. Stir
in the vanilla extract. Set the batter aside
in a cool place for up to half an hour.

4 Apply a light, even coat of spray oil to
an 18cm/7in non-stick frying pan. Whisk
the batter, then pour a little of it into the
hot pan, swirling to cover the base of the
pan evenly. Cook until the mixture comes
away from the sides and the crêpe is
golden underneath.

5 Flip the crêpe over with a large palette
knife and cook the other side briefly until
golden. Slide the crêpe on to a heatproof
plate. Make seven more crêpes in the
same way. Cover the crêpes with foil or
another plate and keep them hot in a
warm oven.

COOK'S TIP

For safety, when igniting a mixture for
flambéing, use a long taper or long
wooden match. Stand back as you set
the mixture alight.

6 To prepare the fruit, melt the spread in
a frying pan, stir in the sugar and cook
gently. Add the orange juice and rind
and cook until syrupy.

7 Add the fruits and warm through
(keeping some back for decoration), then
add the liqueur and set it alight.

8 Fold the pancakes into quarters and
arrange two on each plate. Spoon over the
fruit mixture and dust with icing sugar.
Serve the remaining fruit separately.

NUTRITIONAL NOTES

Per portion:

Energy	285Kcals/1203kJ
Fat, total	5g
Saturated fat	1.06g
Cholesterol	59.5mg
Fibre	3.5g

BLUEBERRY AND ORANGE CRÊPE BASKETS

Impress your guests with these pretty, fruit-filled crêpes. When blueberries are out of season, use other soft fruit, such as raspberries or blackberries.

INGREDIENTS
*150g/5oz/1¼ cups plain
(all-purpose) flour
pinch of salt
2 egg whites
200ml/7fl oz/scant 1 cup skimmed
(very low-fat) milk
150ml/¼ pint/⅔ cup orange juice
spray oil, for greasing*

FOR THE FILLING
*4 medium oranges
225g/8oz/2 cups blueberries*

SERVES 6

NUTRITIONAL NOTES
Per portion:

Energy	165Kcals/697kJ
Fat, total	1.4g
Saturated fat	0.16g
Cholesterol	0.7mg
Fibre	3.2g

1 Preheat the oven to 200°C/400°F/Gas 6.

2 Sift the flour and salt into a bowl. Make a well in the centre and add the egg whites, milk and orange juice. Beat, gradually incorporating the flour mixture, then whisk until the batter is smooth.

3 Apply a light, even coat of spray oil to a heavy pancake pan and heat it. Wait until the oil is very hot, then pour in just enough batter to cover the base of the pan, swirling it to cover the pan evenly.

4 Cook until the pancake has set and is golden on the underside, and then carefully turn it to cook on the other side. Watch it carefully because the second side will cook more quickly than the first and will burn easily.

5 Slide the pancake on to a sheet of kitchen paper. Cook the remaining batter, to make six pancakes.

6 Invert six small ovenproof bowls or moulds on a baking sheet and drape a pancake over each. Bake them in the oven for about 10 minutes, until they are crisp and set into shape. Carefully lift the "baskets" off the moulds.

7 Pare a thin piece of orange rind from one orange and cut it in fine strips. Blanch the strips in boiling water for 30 seconds, rinse them in cold water and drain them on kitchen paper. Cut all the peel and white pith from all the oranges.

8 Cut the oranges into segments, working over a bowl to catch the juice.

9 Add the segments and juice to the blueberries in a pan and warm gently.

10 Spoon the fruit into the baskets and scatter the shreds of rind over the top.

COOK'S TIP
Don't fill the pancake baskets until you are ready to serve them, because they will absorb the fruit juice and begin to soften.

HAZELNUT PAVLOVA

—

**A hint of hazelnut gives the meringue a marvellous flavour, and provides a great contrast
to the luscious summer fruit and light soft cheese topping.**

INGREDIENTS

3 egg whites
175g/6oz/3/4 cup caster (superfine) sugar
5ml/1 tsp cornflour (cornstarch)
5ml/1 tsp white wine vinegar
20g/3/4 oz/3 tbsp roasted hazelnuts,
chopped
250g/9oz/1 cup low-fat cream cheese
15ml/1 tbsp fresh orange juice
30ml/2 tbsp low-fat natural (plain) yogurt
2 ripe nectarines, stoned (pitted)
and sliced
225g/8oz/2 cups raspberries, halved
15ml/1 tbsp redcurrant jelly, warmed

SERVES 4–6

1 Preheat the oven to 140°C/275°F/Gas 1.
Lightly grease a baking sheet.

2 Draw a 20cm/8in circle on a sheet of
baking parchment. Place the paper
pencil-side down on the baking sheet.
Check the circle is visible.

3 Place the egg whites in a clean, grease-
free bowl and whisk until stiff. Add the
sugar 15ml/1 tbsp at a time, whisking
well after each addition.

4 Add the cornflour, vinegar and
hazelnuts and fold in carefully with a
large metal spoon.

5 Spoon the meringue on to the marked
circle and spread out to the edges,
making a dip in the centre.

6 Bake for about 1¼–1½ hours, until
crisp and dry. Leave to cool slightly, then
transfer to a wire rack to go completely
cold. Transfer to a serving platter.

7 Beat the soft cheese and orange juice
together, stir in the yogurt and spoon on
to the meringue. Top with the fruit and
drizzle over the warmed redcurrant jelly.
Serve immediately.

NUTRITIONAL NOTES
Per portion:

Energy	332Kcals/1402kJ
Fat, total	4.4g
Saturated fat	0.82g
Cholesterol	0.3mg
Fibre	2.6g

PINEAPPLE AND STRAWBERRY MERINGUE

—

**This is a gooey meringue that doesn't usually hold a perfect shape, but it has a
wonderful marshmallow texture. It's a perfect sweet treat.**

INGREDIENTS

5 egg whites, at room temperature
pinch of salt
5ml/1 tsp cornflour (cornstarch)
15ml/1 tbsp distilled malt vinegar
few drops of vanilla extract
*275g/10oz/1¼ cups caster
(superfine) sugar*
*250ml/8fl oz/1 cup low-fat Greek
(US strained plain) yogurt*
175g/6oz fresh pineapple, cut into chunks
175g/6oz/1⅓ cups fresh strawberries
strawberry leaves, to decorate (optional)

SERVES 6

1 Preheat the oven to 160°C/325°F/
Gas 3. Line a baking sheet with non-stick
baking paper.

2 Whisk the egg whites in a grease-free
bowl until they hold stiff peaks. Add the
salt, cornflour, vinegar and vanilla
extract; whisk again until stiff.

NUTRITIONAL NOTES
Per portion:

Energy	247Kcals/1050kJ
Fat, total	2.2g
Saturated fat	1.31g
Cholesterol	2.9mg
Fibre	0.7g

3 Gently whisk in half the sugar, then
carefully fold in the rest.

4 Spoon the meringue on to the baking
sheet and swirl into a 20cm/8in round
with the back of a large spoon.

5 Bake for 20 minutes, then reduce the
oven temperature to 150°C/300°F/Gas 2
and bake for 40 minutes more.

6 Transfer the meringue to a serving
plate, then leave to cool.

7 To serve, top with Greek yogurt,
pineapple chunks and halved
strawberries. Decorate with leaves.

COOK'S TIP
You can also cook this in a deep,
20cm/8in loose-base cake tin. Cover
the base with baking parchment and
grease the sides.

NECTARINE AND HAZELNUT MERINGUES
—

If it's indulgence you're seeking, look no further. Sweet nectarines and yogurt paired with crisp hazelnut meringues make a superb sweet.

3 Fold in two-thirds of the hazelnuts, then spoon five ovals on to each baking sheet. Scatter the remaining hazelnuts over five of the meringues.

4 Bake for 1–1¼ hours until dry. Put on a wire rack to go cold.

5 Mix the Greek yogurt with the dessert wine. Spoon some on to each plain meringue. Arrange a few nectarine slices on each. Put each meringue on a plate with a hazelnut-topped meringue. Decorate with mint and serve at once.

INGREDIENTS
3 egg whites
175g/6oz/¾ cup caster (superfine) sugar
50g/2oz/½ cup chopped hazelnuts, toasted
300ml/½ pint/1¼ cups low-fat Greek (US strained plain) yogurt
15ml/1 tbsp sweet dessert wine
2 nectarines, stoned (pitted) and sliced
fresh mint sprigs, to decorate

SERVES 5

1 Preheat the oven to 140°C/275°F/Gas 1. Line two large baking sheets with non-stick baking paper.

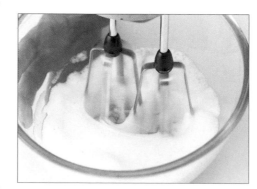

2 Whisk the egg whites in a grease-free bowl until they form stiff peaks. Whisk in the caster sugar a spoonful at a time until the mixture forms a stiff, glossy meringue.

VARIATIONS
Use apricots instead of nectarines if you prefer.

NUTRITIONAL NOTES
Per portion:

Energy	293Kcals/1236kJ
Fat, total	4.9g
Saturated fat	2.34g
Cholesterol	4.2mg
Fibre	1.4g

SOFT FRUIT PAVLOVA

There is rather a lot of sugar in meringue, but for special occasions this is the queen of desserts
and a practical way of using up leftover egg whites.

INGREDIENTS
low-fat oil, for oiling
4 egg whites
175g/6oz/³/4 cup caster (superfine) sugar
30ml/2 tbsp redcurrant jelly
15ml/1 tbsp rose water
300ml/¹/2 pint/1¹/4 cups low-fat
Greek (US strained plain) yogurt
450g/1lb/4 cups mixed soft fruits berries
10ml/2 tsp icing (confectioners')
sugar, sifted
pinch salt

SERVES 4

1 Preheat the oven to 140°C/275°F/Gas 1.
Oil a baking sheet.

2 Whisk the egg whites with a pinch of
salt in a clean, grease-free bowl, until
stiff. Slowly add the caster sugar and
keep whisking until the mixture forms
stiff, glossy peaks.

NUTRITIONAL NOTES
Per portion:

Energy	302Kcals/1280kJ
Fat, total	3.9g
Saturated fat	2.37g
Cholesterol	5.3mg
Fibre	3.1g

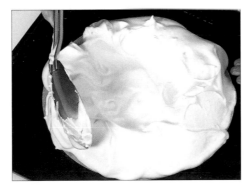

3 Spoon the meringue into a 25cm/10in
round on the baking sheet, making a
slight indentation in the centre.

4 Bake for 1–1¹/2 hours until the
meringue is firm. Keep checking as the
meringue can easily overcook. Transfer
the meringue to a serving plate.

5 Melt the redcurrant jelly in a small
heatproof bowl resting in a pan of hot
water. Cool slightly, then spread in the
centre of the meringue.

6 Mix the rose water with the yogurt and
spoon on top. Arrange the fruits on top
and dust lightly with the icing sugar.

CUSTARDS, SOUFFLÉS, WHIPS AND CAKES

Creamy and light, yet satisfying and full of flavour, the dishes in this chapter are ideal to serve

after a rich main course to refresh the taste buds with tantalizing flavours, and provide a sweet

flavour. All are quick to prepare and use minimal ingredients, so choose the best quality that you

can afford. Presentation is everything with simple desserts, so take your time. If your choice

is for a more substantial dessert, this chapter also contains recipes for cakes and cheesecakes.

Dishes such as these are perfect for lavish entertaining or other special occasions and no-one will

know that what they're eating is a low-fat and healthy version of a traditional dessert.

TOFU BERRY BRÛLÉE

Brûlée is usually out-of-bounds on a low-fat diet, but this version is perfectly acceptable,
as it uses tofu, which is low in fat and free from cholesterol.

INGREDIENTS

300g/11oz packet silken tofu
45ml/3 tbsp icing (confectioners') sugar
225g/8oz/2 cups red berry fruits, such as
raspberries, strawberries and redcurrants
about 75ml/5 tbsp demerara (raw) sugar

SERVES 4

NUTRITIONAL NOTES
Per portion:

Energy	180Kcals/760kJ
Fat, total	3.01g
Saturated fat	0.41g
Cholesterol	0mg
Fibre	1.31g

1 Mix the tofu and icing sugar in a
food processor or blender and process
until smooth.

COOK'S TIP
Choose silken tofu as it gives a
smoother texture than firm tofu in this
type of dish. Silken tofu is used for
sauces, sweet dishes and desserts
because it gives a rich and creamy
texture to food. Firm tofu is better for
cooking in chunks.

2 Stir the berry fruits into the blended
mixture, then spoon them into a
900ml/1½ pint/3¾ cup flameproof dish.
Flatten the top.

3 Sprinkle the top with enough sugar
to cover evenly. Place under a
very hot grill until the sugar melts and
caramelizes. Chill before serving.

POPPYSEED CUSTARD WITH RED FRUIT

Poppyseeds add a nutty flavour to this creamy custard without increasing
the amount of fat too much. This is comfort eating at its best.

INGREDIENTS
low-fat spread, for greasing
600ml/1 pint/2¹/2 cups skimmed
(very low-fat) milk
2 eggs
15ml/1 tbsp caster (superfine) sugar
15ml/1 tbsp poppyseeds
115g/4oz/1 cup each of strawberries,
raspberries and blackberries
15ml/1 tbsp soft light brown sugar
60ml/4 tbsp red grape juice

SERVES 6

1 Preheat the oven to 150°C/300°F/Gas 2.
Lightly grease a soufflé dish.

2 Beat the eggs in a bowl with the caster
sugar and poppyseeds until creamy.

3 Heat the milk until just below boiling
point. Whisk the milk into the egg
mixture.

4 Stand the soufflé dish in a shallow
roasting tin, and pour in hot water to
come halfway up the sides of the dish.

VARIATION
Omit the poppyseeds and sprinkle the
custard surface with grated nutmeg.

5 Pour the custard into the soufflé dish.

6 Bake for 50–60 minutes, until the
custard is just set and golden on top.

7 Meanwhile, mix the fruit with the
soft brown sugar and fruit juice. Chill
until ready to serve with the warm
baked custard.

NUTRITIONAL NOTES
Per portion:

Energy	109Kcals/460kJ
Fat, total	3.1g
Saturated fat	0.69g
Cholesterol	66.2mg
Fibre	1.3g

PASSION FRUIT BRÛLÉE

Fruit brûlées are usually made with double cream, but Greek yogurt works just as well. The brown sugar required for this recipe is reserved for the crunchy caramelized topping.

INGREDIENTS
4 passion fruit
300ml/¹/₂ pint/1¹/₄ cups low-fat
Greek (US strained plain) yogurt
75g/3oz/¹/₂ cup soft light brown sugar
15ml/1 tbsp water

SERVES 4

NUTRITIONAL NOTES
Per portion:

Energy	139Kcals/590kJ
Fat, total	3.8g
Saturated fat	2.37g
Cholesterol	5.3mg
Fibre	0.5g

1 Cut the passion fruit in half. Use a teaspoon to scoop out all the pulp and seeds. Divide the fruit among four ovenproof ramekins.

2 Spoon equal amounts of the yogurt on top of the fruit and smooth the surface level. Chill for at least 2 hours.

3 Put the sugar in a small pan with the water and heat gently, stirring, until the sugar has melted and caramelized.

4 Pour over the yogurt; the caramel will harden within 1 minute. Serve immediately or keep in a cool place until required.

MANGO AND GINGER CLOUDS

The sweet, perfumed flavour of ripe mango combines beautifully with ginger, and this low-fat, light and airy dessert makes the best of both flavours.

INGREDIENTS

3 ripe mangoes
3 pieces stem ginger, plus 45ml/3 tbsp
syrup from the jar
75g/3oz/¹/2 cup silken tofu
3 egg whites
6 unsalted pistachio nuts, chopped

SERVES 6

3 Whisk the egg whites in a grease-free bowl until they form soft peaks. Fold them lightly into the mango mixture.

4 Spoon the mixture into wide dishes or glasses and chill before serving, sprinkled with the chopped pistachios.

NUTRITIONAL NOTES
Per portion:

Energy	141Kcals/592kJ
Fat, total	1.9g
Saturated fat	0.21g
Cholesterol	0mg
Fibre	3.9g

1 Cut the mangoes' flesh off the stone, remove the peel and chop the flesh.

2 Put the mango flesh in a food processor and add the ginger, syrup and tofu. Process until smooth. Spoon into a bowl.

NOTE
Raw or lightly cooked egg whites should be avoided by women during pregnancy, as well as young children and the elderly.

RASPBERRY PASSION FRUIT SWIRLS

If passion fruit is not available, this simple-to-make dessert can be made with
raspberries alone. You could add a squeeze of fresh lime juice for a fresh taste.

4 Place alternate spoonfuls of the
raspberry pulp and the fromage frais
mixture into stemmed glasses or
serving dishes.

INGREDIENTS
300g/11oz/2¹/₂ cups raspberries
2 passion fruit
*400ml/14fl oz/1²/₃ cups low-fat
fromage frais*
30ml/2 tbsp caster (superfine) sugar
*raspberries and fresh mint sprigs,
to decorate*

SERVES 4

1 Using a fork, mash the raspberries in a
small bowl until the juice runs.

2 Place the fromage frais and sugar in a
separate bowl.

3 Halve the passion fruit and scoop out
the seeds. Add to the fromage frais and
mix well.

5 Stir lightly to create a swirled effect.

6 Decorate each dessert with a whole
raspberry and a sprig of fresh mint.
Serve chilled.

COOK'S TIP
Over-ripe, slightly soft fruit can be
used in this recipe. Use frozen
raspberries when fresh are not
available, but thaw them first.

NUTRITIONAL NOTES
Per portion:

Energy	110Kcals/462kJ
Fat, total	0.47g
Saturated fat	0.13g
Cholesterol	1mg
Fibre	2.12g

GOOSEBERRY CHEESE COOLER

Gooseberries are one of the less common summer fruits and are only in season for a short time,
so they're well worth snapping up when you can get them.

INGREDIENTS
450g/1lb/4 cups fresh or frozen
gooseberries
1 small orange
15ml/1 tbsp clear honey
250g/9oz/1 cup low-fat cottage cheese

SERVES 4

NUTRITIONAL NOTES
Per portion:

Energy	93Kcals/392kJ
Fat, total	1.4g
Saturated fat	0.56g
Cholesterol	3.1mg
Fibre	3.4g

1 Top and tail the gooseberries and place them in a medium pan.

2 Finely grate the orange and squeeze the juice; then add the rind and juice to the pan. Cover the pan and cook gently, stirring occasionally, until the fruit is completely tender.

3 Remove from the heat and stir in the honey. Purée the gooseberries with the cooking liquid in a food processor until almost smooth. Allow to cool.

4 Press the cottage cheese through a sieve, or process it in a food processor, until smooth. Stir half the cooled gooseberry purée into the cheese.

5 Spoon the cheese mixture into four serving dishes or glasses. Top each with a spoonful of the gooseberry purée. Serve chilled.

STRAWBERRY ROSE-PETAL PASHKA

—

This lighter version of a traditional Russian dessert is ideal for dinner parties – make it a day or two in advance for best results.

INGREDIENTS
350g/12oz/1½ cups low-fat cottage cheese
175ml/6fl oz/¾ cup low-fat
natural (plain) yogurt
30ml/2 tbsp clear honey
2.5ml/½ tsp rose-water
275g/10oz/2½ cups strawberries
handful of scented pink rose petals,
to decorate

SERVES 4

VARIATION
Use small porcelain heart-shaped
moulds with draining holes for a
pretty alternative.

---

1 Drain any free liquid from the cottage cheese and tip the cheese into a sieve. Use a wooden spoon to rub it through the sieve into a bowl. Stir the yogurt, honey and rose-water into the cheese.

2 Roughly chop about half the strawberries and fold them into the cheese mixture.

3 Line a new, clean flowerpot or a sieve with fine muslin and tip the cheese mixture in. Leave it to drain over a bowl for several hours, or overnight.

4 Invert the flowerpot or sieve on to a serving plate, turn out the pashka and lift off the muslin. Chill at this point if not serving straightaway.

5 Cut the remaining strawberries in half and arrange them around the pashka. Scatter the rose petals over. Serve chilled.

NUTRITIONAL NOTES
Per portion:

Energy	133Kcals/561kJ
Fat, total	1.6g
Saturated fat	1g
Cholesterol	6.1mg
Fibre	0.8g

PEACH AND GINGER PASHKA

—

This is a low-fat version of the Russian Easter favourite, made with peaches and stem ginger. It's a perfect choice after a rich or heavier main course.

INGREDIENTS

350g/12oz/1½ cups low-fat cottage cheese
2 ripe peaches or nectarines
90g/3½oz/scant ½ cup low-fat
natural (plain) yogurt
2 pieces stem ginger in syrup, drained and
chopped, plus 30ml/2 tbsp syrup
from the jar
2.5ml/½ tsp vanilla extract

TO DECORATE

1 peach or nectarine, peeled and sliced
10ml/2 tsp flaked (slivered)
almonds, toasted

SERVES 4

1 Drain the cottage cheese and rub it through a sieve into a bowl. Stone and roughly chop the peaches or nectarines.

2 In a bowl, mix together the fruit, cottage cheese, yogurt, stem ginger, syrup and vanilla.

3 Line a new, clean flower pot or a strainer with a piece of clean, fine cloth such as cheesecloth.

4 Tip in the cheese mixture, wrap over the cloth and weight down. Leave over a bowl in a cool place to drain overnight. Unwrap the cloth and invert the pashka on to a plate. Decorate with fruit slices and almonds.

NUTRITIONAL NOTES
Per portion:

Energy	147Kcals/621kJ
Fat, total	2.9g
Saturated fat	0.89g
Cholesterol	5.3mg
Fibre	1.1g

COOK'S TIP
Rather than making one large pashka, line four to six cups or ramekins with the clean cloth or muslin and divide the mixture among them.

LEMON HEARTS WITH STRAWBERRY SAUCE

These elegant little hearts are perfect for a romantic celebration. Make them ahead of time for
best results and to allow the dessert to set in the moulds.

INGREDIENTS
175g/6oz/3/4 cup low-fat cottage cheese
*150ml/1/4 pint/2/3 cup half-fat
crème fraîche*
15ml/1 tbsp sugar
finely grated rind of 1/2 lemon
30ml/2 tbsp lemon juice
10ml/2 tsp powdered gelatine
2 egg whites
low-fat spread, for greasing

FOR THE SAUCE
*225g/8oz/2 cups fresh or frozen and
thawed strawberries, plus extra to decorate*
15ml/1 tbsp lemon juice

SERVES 6

1 Press the cottage cheese through a
sieve into a bowl. Beat in the crème
fraîche, sugar and lemon rind.

2 Pour the lemon juice into a small
heatproof bowl and sprinkle the powdered
gelatine over the surface. When it is
sponge-like, place the bowl over a pan
of hot water and stir to dissolve the
gelatine completely.

3 Quickly stir the gelatine into the
cheese mixture, mixing it in evenly.

4 Beat the egg whites in a grease-free
bowl until they form soft peaks. Fold
them into the cheese mixture before it
starts to set.

5 Spoon the mixture into six greased,
heart-shaped moulds, and chill until set.

6 To make the sauce, process the
strawberries and lemon juice in a food
processor until smooth. Pour on to serving
plates and invert the lemon hearts on top.
Decorate with slices of strawberry.

COOK'S TIP
If you don't have heart-shaped, use
individual fluted moulds.

NUTRITIONAL NOTES
Per portion:

Energy	94Kcals/397kJ
Fat, total	4.2g
Saturated fat	2.60g
Cholesterol	27.7mg
Fibre	0.4g

FLUFFY BANANA AND PINEAPPLE SOUFFLÉ

This light, low-fat mousse looks very impressive and, even better, is really very easy to make, especially with a food processor.

INGREDIENTS
2 ripe bananas
225g/8oz/1 cup low-fat cottage cheese
425g/15oz can pineapple chunks or
pieces in juice
60ml/4 tbsp water
15ml/1 tbsp powdered gelatine
2 egg whites

SERVES 6

1 Tie a double band of non-stick baking parchment around a 600ml/1 pint/ 2½ cup soufflé dish, to come approximately 5cm/2in above the rim.

2 Peel and chop one banana and place it in a food processor with the cottage cheese. Process the mixture until smooth.

3 Drain the pineapple and reserve a few pieces for decoration. Add the rest of the pineapple to the mixture in the processor and process until finely chopped.

4 Pour the water into a small heatproof bowl and sprinkle the gelatine on top. Leave until spongy, then place the bowl over hot water, stirring occasionally, until all the gelatine has dissolved.

5 Whisk the egg whites in a grease-free bowl until they hold soft peaks, then fold them lightly and evenly into the mixture.

6 Tip the mixture into the prepared dish, smooth the surface and chill it in the refrigerator, until set.

7 When the soufflé has set, carefully remove the paper collar. Decorate the soufflé with the reserved slices of banana and chunks of pineapple.

NUTRITIONAL NOTES
Per portion:

Energy	106Kcals/452kJ
Fat, total	0.6g
Saturated fat	0.37g
Cholesterol	1.9mg
Fibre	0.7g

QUICK APRICOT BLENDER WHIP

One of the quickest desserts you could make – and also one of the prettiest
with its delicate swirl of creamy apricot.

INGREDIENTS

400g/14oz can apricot halves in juice
15ml/1 tbsp Grand Marnier or brandy
175ml/6fl oz/3/4 cup low-fat Greek
(US strained plain) yogurt
15ml/1 tbsp flaked (slivered) almonds

SERVES 4

1 Drain the juice from the apricots and
place the fruit and liqueur in a blender
or food processor.

2 Process the apricots until smooth.

NUTRITIONAL NOTES

Per portion:

Energy	88Kcals/369kJ
Fat, total	4.4g
Saturated fat	1.38g
Cholesterol	3.1mg
Fibre	0.9g

3 Alternately spoon fruit purée and
yogurt into four tall glasses or glass
dishes, swirling them together slightly
to give a marbled effect.

4 Lightly toast the almonds until they are
golden. Let them cool slightly and then
sprinkle them on top of each whip. Serve
at once.

APRICOT DELIGHT

A fluffy mousse base with a layer of fruit jelly on top makes this dessert doubly delicious.
Fructose is a sweetener, available in larger supermarkets.

INGREDIENTS
2 × 400g/14oz cans apricots in
natural juice
60ml/4 tbsp fructose
15ml/1 tbsp lemon juice
25ml/1¹/2 tbsp powdered gelatine
425g/15oz low fat ready-to-serve custard
150ml/¹/4 pint/²/3 cup low-fat natural
(plain) yogurt, strained

TO DECORATE
whipped cream
1 apricot, sliced
1 sprig of fresh apple mint

SERVES 8

1 Line the base of a 1.2 litre/2 pint/5 cup heart-shaped or round cake tin (pan) with baking parchment (not a loose-base tin).

2 Drain the apricots, reserving the juice. Put the drained apricots in a food processor or blender. Add the fructose and 60ml/4 tbsp of the apricot juice. Blend to a smooth purée.

3 Measure 30ml/2 tbsp of the apricot juice into a small bowl. Add the lemon juice, then sprinkle over 10ml/2 tsp of the gelatine. Leave for 5 minutes, until spongy.

4 Stir the gelatine into half the apricot purée and pour into the tin. Chill in the refrigerator for 1¹/2 hours, or until firm.

5 Sprinkle the remaining 15ml/1 tbsp gelatine over 60ml/4 tbsp of the apricot juice. Soak and dissolve as before. Mix the remaining apricot purée with the custard, yogurt and gelatine. Pour on to the layer of set fruit purée and chill in the refrigerator for 3 hours.

6 Dip the cake tin into hot water for a few seconds and unmould the delice on to a serving plate. Decorate with whipped cream, the sliced apricot and a sprig of fresh apple mint.

NUTRITIONAL NOTES
Per portion:

Energy	155Kcals/649kJ
Fat, total	0.63g
Saturated fat	0.33g
Cholesterol	0mg
Fibre	0.9g

RASPBERRY VACHERIN

Meringue rounds filled with orange-flavoured fromage frais and fresh raspberries
make a perfect dinner-party dessert.

INGREDIENTS
3 egg whites
175g/6oz/3/4 cup caster (superfine) sugar
5ml/1 tsp chopped almonds
icing (confectioners') sugar, for dusting
raspberry leaves, to decorate (optional)

FOR THE FILLING
175g/6oz/3/4 cup low-fat soft cheese
15ml/1 tbsp clear honey
15ml/1 tbsp orange liqueur
120ml/4fl oz/1/2 cup low-fat fromage frais
225g/8oz/2 cups raspberries

SERVES 6

1 Preheat the oven to 140°C/275°F/Gas 1.

2 Draw a 20cm/8in circle on each of two pieces of non-stick baking paper. Turn the papers over so the marking is on the underside and use them to line two heavy baking sheets.

NUTRITIONAL NOTES
Per portion:

Energy	248Kcals/1041kJ
Fat, total	2.22g
Saturated fat	0.82g
Cholesterol	4mg
Fibre	1.06g

3 Whisk the egg whites in a grease-free bowl until very stiff, then gradually whisk in the caster sugar to make a stiff meringue mixture.

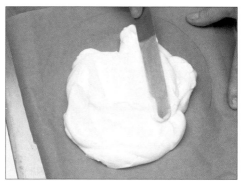

4 Spoon the meringue on to the circles on the prepared baking sheets, spreading it out evenly to the edges. Sprinkle one meringue round with the chopped almonds.

5 Bake for 1½–2 hours, then lift the meringue rounds off the baking sheets, peel away the paper and cool on a wire rack.

6 To make the filling, beat the soft cheese with the honey and liqueur in a bowl. Fold in the fromage frais and raspberries, reserving three of the best raspberries for decoration.

7 Place the plain meringue round on a board, carefully spread with the filling and top with the nut-covered round.

8 Dust with icing sugar, transfer to a serving plate and decorate with the reserved raspberries, and a sprig of raspberry leaves, if you like.

COOK'S TIP
When making the meringue, whisk the egg whites until they are so stiff that you can turn the bowl upside-down without them falling out.

ANGEL CAKE

Serve this light-as-air, white crumb cake with low-fat fromage frais – it makes a
perfect dessert or tea-time treat, when you're in need of something sweet to eat.

4 Gently fold in the flour mixture with
a large metal spoon.

5 Spoon into an ungreased 25cm/10in
angel cake tin, smooth the surface and
bake for about 45–50 minutes, until the
cake springs back when lightly pressed.

6 Sprinkle a sheet of baking parchment
with caster sugar and set an egg cup in
the centre. Invert the cake tin over the
paper, balancing it carefully on the egg
cup. When cold, the cake will drop out of
the tin. Transfer it to a plate, decorate if
liked, then dust with icing sugar.

INGREDIENTS

40g/1¹/₂ oz/¹/₃ cup cornflour (cornstarch)
40g/1¹/₂ oz/¹/₃ cup plain (all-purpse) flour
8 egg whites
225g/8oz/1 cup caster (superfine) sugar,
plus extra for sprinkling
5ml/1 tsp pure vanilla extract
icing (confectioners') sugar, for dusting

SERVES 10

NUTRITIONAL NOTES
Per portion:

Energy	139Kcals/582kJ
Fat, total	0.08g
Saturated fat	0.01g
Cholesterol	0mg
Fibre	0.13g

1 Preheat the oven to 180°C/350°F/
Gas 4.

2 Sift both flours on to a sheet of
baking parchment.

3 Whisk the egg whites in a clean
grease-free bowl until very stiff, then
gradually add the sugar and vanilla
extract, whisking until the mixture is
thick and glossy.

COOK'S TIP
Make a lemony icing by mixing
175g/6oz/1¹/₂ cups icing sugar with
15–30ml/1–2 tbsp lemon juice. Drizzle
over the cake and decorate with physalis.

TOFU BERRY CHEESECAKE

—

This summery "cheesecake" makes a light and refreshing finish to any meal. Strictly speaking, it isn't a cheesecake at all, as it is based on tofu – but who would guess?

INGREDIENTS
FOR THE BASE
30ml/2 tbsp low-fat spread
30ml/2 tbsp unsweetened apple juice
115g/4oz/2¹/2 cups bran flakes or other high-fibre cereal

FOR THE FILLING
275g/10oz/1¹/2 cups silken tofu
250ml/8fl oz/1 cup low-fat natural (plain) yogurt
60ml/4 tbsp apple juice
15ml/1 tbsp powdered gelatine

FOR THE TOPPING
175g/6oz/1¹/2 cups mixed summer soft fruit, such as strawberries, raspberries, redcurrants and blackberries
30ml/2 tbsp redcurrant jelly
30ml/2 tbsp hot water

SERVES 6

1 For the base, place the low-fat spread and apple juice in a pan and heat them gently until the spread has melted.

2 Crush the cereal and stir it into the pan, mixing well.

3 Tip the crushed cereal into a 23cm/9in round flan tin and press down firmly. Leave to set.

4 To make the filling, place the tofu and yogurt in a food processor and process until smooth.

5 Pour the apple juice into a small bowl. Sprinkle the gelatine on top. Leave until spongy, then stand over hot water until melted. Stir quickly into the tofu mixture.

6 Spread the tofu mixture over the chilled base. Chill until set. Remove the flan tin and place the "cheesecake" on a serving plate.

7 Arrange the fruits over the top. Melt the redcurrant jelly with the hot water. Let it cool, then spoon over the fruit to serve.

NUTRITIONAL NOTES
Per portion:

Energy	163Kcals/688kJ
Fat, total	4.4g
Saturated fat	0.93g
Cholesterol	1.6mg
Fibre	3.2g

PEACH SWISS ROLL

A feather-light, low-fat, sponge with a filling of peach jam – delicious at tea time
or as a dinner-party dessert to impress your friends.

INGREDIENTS

low-fat spread, for greasing
3 eggs
115g/4oz/1/2 cup caster (superfine) sugar
75g/3oz/3/4 cup plain (all-purpose)
flour, sifted
15ml/1 tbsp boiling water
90ml/6 tbsp peach jam
icing (confectioners') sugar,
for dusting (optional)

SERVES 6–8

NUTRITIONAL NOTES
Per portion:

Energy	178Kcals/746kJ
Fat, total	2.45g
Saturated fat	0.67g
Cholesterol	82.5mg
Fibre	0.33g

1 Preheat the oven to 200°C/400°F/ Gas 6. Grease a 30 × 20cm/12 × 8in Swiss roll tin (jelly roll pan) and line with baking parchment.

2 Combine the eggs and sugar in a bowl. Whisk until thick and mousse-like (when the whisk is lifted, a trail should remain on the surface of the mixture for at least 15 seconds).

3 Fold in the flour with a metal spoon. Add the boiling water in the same way.

4 Spoon into the prepared tin, spread evenly to the edges and bake for about 10–12 minutes.

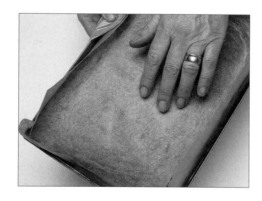

5 The cake should spring back when lightly pressed.

6 Spread a sheet of baking parchment on a flat surface, sprinkle with caster sugar, then invert the cake on top. Peel off the lining paper.

7 Trim the edges of the cake. Make a neat cut two-thirds of the way through the cake, about 1cm/1/2in from the short edge nearest you.

8 Spread the cake with the peach jam and roll up quickly from the partially cut end. Hold in position for a minute, making sure the join is underneath. Cool on a wire rack.

9 Decorate with glacé icing (see Cook's Tip) or dust with icing sugar before serving.

COOK'S TIP
Decorate the Swiss roll with glacé icing. Put 115g/4oz glacé icing in a piping bag fitted with a small writing nozzle and pipe lines over the top of the Swiss roll.

LEMON CHIFFON CAKE

Lemon mousse provides a tangy filling for this light lemon sponge,
which is simple to prepare.

INGREDIENTS
low-fat spread, for greasing
2 eggs
75g/3oz/6 tbsp caster (superfine) sugar
grated rind of 1 lemon
50g/2oz/¹/2 cup plain (all-purpose)
flour, sifted
thinly pared lemon rind, cut in shreds

FOR THE FILLING
2 eggs, separated
75g/3oz/6 tbsp caster (superfine) sugar
grated rind and juice of 1 lemon
30ml/2 tbsp water
15ml/1 tbsp powdered gelatine
120ml/4fl oz/¹/2 cup low-fat fromage frais

FOR THE ICING
115g/4oz/1 cup icing (confectioners')
sugar, sifted
15ml/1 tbsp lemon juice

SERVES 8

1 Preheat the oven to 180°C/350°F/Gas 4.
Grease and line a 20cm/8in loose-base
cake tin.

2 Whisk the eggs, sugar and lemon rind
until thick and mousse-like. Gently fold
in the flour.

3 Turn the mixture into the prepared tin.

4 Bake for 20–25 minutes until the cake
springs back when lightly pressed in the
centre. Turn on to a wire rack to cool.

5 Once cold, split the cake in half
horizontally and return the lower half to
the clean cake tin. Set aside.

6 To make the filling, put the egg yolks,
sugar, lemon rind and juice in a bowl.
Beat until thick, pale and creamy.

7 Pour the water into a small heatproof
bowl and sprinkle the gelatine on top.
Leave until spongy, then place over
simmering water and stir until dissolved.
Cool slightly.

8 Whisk the gelatine into the yolk
mixture. Fold in the fromage frais. When
the mixture begins to set, quickly whisk
the egg whites to soft peaks. Fold a
spoonful into the mousse mixture to
lighten it, then fold in the rest.

9 Pour the lemon mousse over the sponge
in the cake tin, spreading it to the edges.
Set the second layer of sponge on top and
chill until set.

10 Slide a palette knife between the tin
and the cake to loosen it, then transfer to
a serving plate. Make the icing by adding
enough lemon juice to the icing sugar to
make a mixture thick enough to coat the
back of a wooden spoon. Pour over the
cake and spread to the edges. Decorate
with the lemon rind.

NUTRITIONAL NOTES
Per portion:

Energy	202Kcals/849kJ
Fat, total	2.81g
Saturated fat	0.79g
Cholesterol	96.41mg
Fibre	0.2g

FRUIT SALADS, ICES AND SORBETS

Cool, fresh and colourful – the wonderful textures and flavours of fruit combine to make interesting salads that are the perfect desserts to follow spicy foods. Indian spices add heat to tropical fruits, Mediterranean fruits are stewed in fortified wine and flavoured in honey, and everyday fruits are combined with herbs and extracts to create winning dessert solutions. Ice creams and sorbets are perfect simply to eat on a hot, sunny afternoon. These take a little more preparation and freezing time, but with careful planning, you should be able to take advantage of fresh summer berries when they are at their most flavourful, and create a luxury treat with minimal fat content.

SPICED FRUIT PLATTER

The spicy sour flavour of the hot and tangy Indian spice chat masala may seem a little strange at
first, but this dessert can become quite addictive!

INGREDIENTS
1 pineapple
2 papayas
1 small melon
juice of 2 limes
2 pomegranates
chat masala, to taste
sprigs of fresh mint, to decorate

SERVES 6

NUTRITIONAL NOTES
Per portion:

Energy	102Kcals/429kJ
Fat, total	0.5g
Saturated fat	0g
Cholesterol	0mg
Fibre	4.8g

1 Peel the pineapple. Remove the core
and any remaining "eyes", then cut the
flesh lengthways into thin wedges.

2 Peel the papayas, cut them in half, and
then into thin wedges.

3 Halve the melon and remove the seeds
from the middle. Cut the melon into thin
wedges and remove and discard the skin
using a sharp knife.

4 Arrange the fruit on six individual
plates and sprinkle with the lime juice.

5 Cut the pomegranates in half and scoop
out the seeds, discarding any pith.

6 Scatter the seeds over the fruit. Serve,
sprinkled with a little chat masala to
taste. Scatter over a few sprigs of mint,
to decorate.

FRESH FIGS WITH HONEY AND WINE

Fresh figs are naturally sweet, and they taste wonderful in a honeyed wine syrup.
Any variety can be used in this recipe, their ripeness determining the cooking time.

INGREDIENTS

450ml/³/4 pint/scant 2 cups dry white wine
75g/3oz/¹/3 cup clear honey
50g/2oz/¹/4 cup caster (superfine) sugar
1 small orange
8 whole cloves
450g/1lb fresh figs
1 cinnamon stick
bay leaves, to decorate

FOR THE SAUCE

300ml/¹/2 pint/1¹/4 cups low-fat
Greek (US strained plain) yogurt
5ml/1 tsp vanilla extract
5ml/1 tsp caster (superfine) sugar

SERVES 6

1 Put the wine, honey and sugar in a heavy pan and heat gently until the sugar dissolves.

2 Stud the orange with the cloves and add to the syrup with the figs and cinnamon. Cover and simmer until the figs are soft. Transfer to a serving dish and cool.

3 Flavour the yogurt with the vanilla and sugar. Spoon it into a serving dish.

4 With a small, sharp knife cut one or two of the figs in half, if you like, to show off their pretty centres. Decorate with the bay leaves and serve with the yogurt.

NUTRITIONAL NOTES
Per portion:

Energy	201Kcals/845kJ
Fat, total	2.7g
Saturated fat	1.58g
Cholesterol	3.5mg
Fibre	1.5g

PERSIAN MELON CUPS

This typical Persian dessert uses delicious, fresh fruits flavoured with rose-water
and a hint of aromatic mint.

3 Reserve four strawberries and slice the rest. Place in a bowl with the melon balls, the peaches, grapes, sugar, rose-water and lemon juice.

4 Pile the fruit into the melon shells and chill in the refrigerator for 2 hours.

5 To serve, sprinkle with crushed ice and decorate each melon shell with a whole strawberry and a sprig of mint.

INGREDIENTS

2 small melons
225g/8oz/2 cups strawberries, sliced
3 peaches, peeled and cut into small cubes
225g/8oz seedless grapes
30ml/2 tbsp caster (superfine) sugar
15ml/1 tbsp rose-water
15ml/1 tbsp lemon juice
crushed ice
4 sprigs of mint, to decorate

SERVES 4

COOK'S TIP

If you don't have a melon baller, scoop
out the melon flesh using a large spoon
and cut into bite-size pieces.

1 Cut the melons in half and remove the seeds.

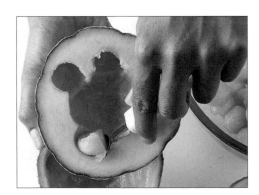

2 Scoop out the flesh with a melon baller, taking care not to damage the skin. Reserve the melon shells for later.

NUTRITIONAL NOTES

Per portion:

Energy	137Kcals/579kJ
Fat, total	0.4g
Saturated fat	0g
Cholesterol	0mg
Fibre	3.2g

STRAWBERRIES WITH COINTREAU

Strawberries at the height of their season are one of summer's greatest pleasures. Try this simple but unusual way of serving them.

INGREDIENTS

1 unwaxed orange
40g/1¹/2 oz/3 tbsp sugar
75ml/5 tbsp water
450g/1lb/3¹/2 cups strawberries, hulled
45ml/3 tbsp Cointreau
250ml/8fl oz/1 cup low-fat Greek
(US strained plain) yogurt

SERVES 4

1 With a vegetable peeler, remove wide strips of rind from the orange, taking care to avoid the pith. Stack two or three strips at a time and cut into very thin julienne strips.

2 Mix the sugar and water in a small pan. Heat gently, swirling the pan occasionally until the sugar has dissolved. Bring to the boil, add the julienne strips, then simmer for 10 minutes. Remove the pan from the heat and leave the syrup to cool completely.

3 Reserve four strawberries for decoration and cut the rest in halves or quarters. Put them in a bowl. Stir the Cointreau or chosen liqueur into the syrup and pour it over the fruit. Add the orange rind. Set aside for at least 30 minutes or for up to 2 hours.

NUTRITIONAL NOTES
Per portion:

Energy	155Kcals/653kJ
Fat, total	3.2g
Saturated fat	1.97g
Cholesterol	4.4mg
Fibre	1.2g

4 Whip the yogurt briefly, then sweeten to taste with a little of the strawberry syrup.

5 Spoon the chopped strawberries into glass serving dishes and top with dollops of the sweetened Greek yogurt. Decorate with the reserved strawberries.

FRESH PINEAPPLE WITH COCONUT

This refreshing dessert can also be made with vacuum-packed pineapple,
and it is very simple to make and light to eat.

INGREDIENTS

*1 fresh pineapple, about
675g/1¹/2 lb, peeled
few slivers of fresh coconut
300ml/¹/2 pint/1¹/4 cups unsweetened
pineapple juice
60ml/4 tbsp coconut liqueur
2.5cm/1in piece stem ginger, plus 45ml/
3 tbsp syrup from the jar*

SERVES 4

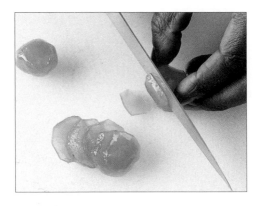

3 Thinly slice the stem ginger and add to
the pan with the ginger syrup. Bring just
to the boil, then simmer gently until the
liquid is slightly reduced and the sauce is
fairly thick.

4 Pour the sauce over the pineapple and
coconut, leave to cool, then chill in the
refrigerator before serving.

1 Peel and slice the pineapple, arrange in
a serving dish and scatter the coconut
slivers on top.

2 Place the pineapple juice and coconut
liqueur in a pan and heat gently.

COOK'S TIP

Coconuts can be stored at room
temperature for six months.

NUTRITIONAL NOTES

Per portion:

Energy	177Kcals/743kJ
Fat, total	2.2g
Saturated fat	1.55g
Cholesterol	0mg
Fibre	2.2g

PERFUMED PINEAPPLE SALAD

This refreshing fruit salad benefits from being prepared ahead. This gives the fruit time to absorb the perfumed flavour of the orange-flower water.

INGREDIENTS
1 small ripe pineapple
15ml/1 tbsp icing (confectioners') sugar
15ml/1 tbsp orange-flower water, or more if liked
115g/4oz/2/3 cup fresh dates, stoned (pitted) and quartered
225g/8oz/2 cups fresh strawberries, sliced
a few fresh mint sprigs, to serve

SERVES 4

1 Cut the skin from the pineapple and, using the tip of a vegetable peeler, remove as many brown "eyes" as possible.

2 Quarter the pineapple lengthways, remove the core from each wedge, then slice.

3 Arrange the pineapple in a shallow serving bowl. Sprinkle with icing sugar and drizzle the orange-flower water over.

NUTRITIONAL NOTES
Per portion:

Energy	127Kcals/534kJ
Fat, total	0.4g
Saturated fat	0g
Cholesterol	0mg
Fibre	2.9g

COOK'S TIP
Orange-flower water is available from good delicatessens.

4 Add the dates and strawberries to the pineapple, cover and chill for at least 2 hours, stirring once or twice. Serve, decorated with a few mint sprigs.

ICED PINEAPPLE CRUSH

The sweet tropical flavours of pineapple and lychees combine well with richly scented
strawberries to make this a most refreshing salad.

INGREDIENTS
2 small pineapples
450g/1lb/4 cups strawberries
400g/14oz can lychees
45ml/3 tbsp kirsch or white rum
30ml/2 tbsp icing (confectioners') sugar

SERVES 4

1 Remove the crown from the pineapples
by twisting sharply. Reserve the leaves
for decoration.

3 Cut around the flesh inside the skin
with a small serrated knife, keeping
the skin intact. Remove the core
from the pineapple.

5 Combine the kirsch or rum with the
icing sugar, pour over the fruit and freeze
for 45 minutes.

2 Cut the fruit in half diagonally with a
large serrated knife.

4 Chop the pineapple and combine with
the strawberries and lychees, taking care
not to damage the fruit.

6 Turn the fruit out into the pineapple
skins and decorate with the leaves.
Serve chilled.

COOK'S TIP
A ripe pineapple will resist pressure
when squeezed and will have a sweet,
fragrant smell. In winter, freezing
conditions can cause the flesh
to blacken.

VARIATION
You could use other tropical fruit such
as mango, pawpaw or guava as well as
the pineapple.

NUTRITIONAL NOTES
Per portion:

Energy	251Kcals/1058kJ
Fat, total	0.7g
Saturated fat	0g
Cholesterol	0mg
Fibre	5.2g

PINEAPPLE WEDGES WITH ALLSPICE AND LIME

Fresh pineapple is easy to prepare and always looks festive, so this dish is
perfect for easy entertaining.

INGREDIENTS

1 ripe pineapple, about 800g/1¾ lb
1 lime
15ml/1 tbsp dark muscovado
(molasses) sugar
5ml/1 tsp ground allspice

SERVES 4

NUTRITIONAL NOTES

Per portion:

Energy	96Kcals/403kJ
Fat, total	0.5g
Saturated fat	0.03g
Cholesterol	0mg
Fibre	2.3g

2 Loosen the flesh on each wedge by
sliding a knife between the flesh and the
skin. Cut the flesh into slices, leaving it
on the skin.

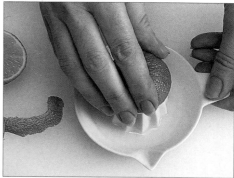

3 Using a canelle knife or sharp-pointed
knife, remove a few shreds of rind from
the lime. Squeeze out the juice.

1 Cut the pineapple lengthways into
quarters and remove the hard central
core from each wedge.

4 Sprinkle the pineapple with the lime
juice and rind, sugar and allspice. Serve
immediately, or chill for up to an hour.

TROPICAL FRUIT MEDLEY WITH ICED YOGURT

Tropical fruit with iced mango yogurt makes a wonderful dessert. Buy very ripe fruit for this dessert, so that it is at its sweetest and juiciest.

INGREDIENTS

2 large ripe mangoes, total weight about 675g/1¹/₂ lb
300ml/¹/₂ pint/1¹/₄ cups low-fat Greek (US strained plain) yogurt
8 dried apricots, halved
150ml/¹/₄ pint/²/₃ cup unsweetened orange juice
1 ripe papaya, about 300g/11oz

SERVES 4

1 Take one thick slice from one of the mangoes and, while still on the skin, slash the flesh with a sharp knife in a criss-cross pattern to make cubes.

2 Turn the piece of mango inside-out and cut away the cubed flesh from the skin. Place in a bowl, mash to a pulp with a fork, then add the Greek yogurt and mix well. Spoon into a freezer tub and freeze for about 1–1¹/₂ hours until half frozen.

3 Meanwhile, put the apricots and orange juice in a small pan. Bring to the boil, then simmer gently until the apricots are soft, adding a little water, if necessary, so that the apricots remain moist. Remove from the heat and set aside to cool.

4 Peel, stone and chop the remaining mangoes. Halve the papaya, remove seeds and peel. Dice the flesh and add to the mango. Pour the apricot sauce on top.

5 Stir the mango yogurt a few times. Serve the fruit topped with the mango yogurt.

NUTRITIONAL NOTES
Per portion:

Energy	231Kcals/967kJ
Fat, total	4.3g
Saturated fat	2.44g
Cholesterol	5.3mg
Fibre	7.5g

PINEAPPLE AND PASSION FRUIT SALSA

Serve this fruity salsa solo or as a filling for halved baby cantaloupes.
Either way it is a cool, refreshing dessert to serve at a dinner party.

INGREDIENTS
1 small fresh pineapple
2 passion fruit
150ml/¼ pint/⅔ cup low-fat
Greek (US strained plain) yogurt
30ml/2 tbsp light muscovado
(brown) sugar
meringues, to serve (optional)

SERVES 6

1 Cut off the top and bottom of the pineapple so that it will stand firmly on a chopping board. Using a large sharp knife, slice off the peel.

2 Use a small sharp knife to carefully cut out the eyes from around the pineapple.

VARIATION
Use low-fat fromage frais instead of the yogurt, if you like.

3 Slice the pineapple and use a small pastry cutter to stamp out the tough core from each slice. Finely chop the flesh.

4 Cut the passion fruit in half and scoop out the seeds and pulp into a bowl.

NUTRITIONAL NOTES
Per portion:

Energy	82Kcals/342kJ
Fat, total	1.5g
Saturated fat	0.79g
Cholesterol	1.8mg
Fibre	1.3g

5 Stir in the chopped pineapple and yogurt. Cover and chill.

6 Stir in the muscovado sugar just before serving the salsa. Serve with meringues, if you like.

COOL GREEN FRUIT SALAD

A sophisticated, simple fruit salad, with a minimal colourscheme, which would look
wonderful served on a bed of crushed ice.

INGREDIENTS
3 Ogen or Galia melons
115g/4oz/1 cup green seedless grapes
2 kiwi fruit
1 star fruit, plus extra slices to garnish
1 green eating apple
1 lime
*175ml/6fl oz/³/4 cup unsweetened
sparkling grape juice*

SERVES 6

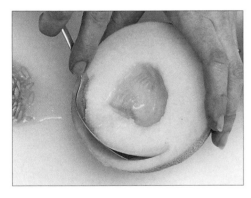

1 Halve the melons and scoop out the
seeds. Keeping the shells intact, scoop
out the flesh and cut into bite-size cubes.
Reserve the melon shells.

2 Cut any large grapes in half. Peel and
chop the kiwi fruit. Slice the star-fruit and
set aside a few slices for decoration.

3 Core and slice the apple and place in a
bowl, with the other fruit.

4 Thinly pare the rind from the lime and
cut it in fine strips. Blanch the strips in
boiling water for 30 seconds, and then
drain them and rinse them in cold water.

NUTRITIONAL NOTES
Per portion:

Energy	91Kcals/382kJ
Fat, total	0.4g
Saturated fat	0.00g
Cholesterol	0.0mg
Fibre	1.6g

5 Squeeze the juice from the lime and
pour it over the fruit. Toss lightly.

6 Spoon the prepared fruit into the
reserved melon shells; chill the shells in
the fridge until required. Just before
serving, spoon the sparkling grape juice
over the fruit and scatter with lime rind.
Decorate with slices of star fruit.

BLUEBERRY AND ORANGE SALAD MERINGUES

What could be prettier than this simple salad composed of delicate blueberries, sharp oranges
and little meringues flavoured with lavender?

INGREDIENTS
6 oranges
350g/12oz/3 cups blueberries
8 sprigs fresh lavender

FOR THE MERINGUE
2 egg whites
115g/4oz/¹/2 cup caster (superfine) sugar
5ml/1 tsp fresh lavender flowers

SERVES 4

1 Preheat the oven to 140°/275°F/
Gas 1. Line a baking sheet with six
layers of newspaper and cover with
baking parchment.

2 Whisk the egg whites in a large grease-
free bowl until they hold soft peaks. Add
the sugar a little at a time, whisking
thoroughly after each addition.

3 Fold in the lavender flowers.

4 Spoon the meringue into a piping bag
fitted with a 5mm/¹/4 in plain nozzle. Pipe
as many small buttons of meringue on to
the prepared baking sheet as you can.
Dry the meringue near the bottom of the
oven for 1¹/2–2 hours.

5 To segment the oranges, remove the
peel from the top, bottom and sides with a
serrated knife. Loosen the segments by
cutting with a paring knife between the
flesh and the membranes, holding the
fruit over a bowl.

6 Arrange the segments on four plates,
fanning them out.

7 Combine the blueberries with the
lavender meringues and pile in the centre
of each plate. Decorate with sprigs of
lavender and serve immediately.

NUTRITIONAL NOTES
Per portion:

Energy	198Kcals/838kJ
Fat, total	0.3g
Saturated fat	0g
Cholesterol	0mg
Fibre	3.5g

COOK'S TIP
Lavender is used in both sweet and
savoury dishes. Always use fresh or
recently dried flowers that are sold for
culinary use, and avoid artificially
scented bunches that are sold for dried
flower displays.

VARIATIONS
• You could use blackberries or firm
raspberries with fresh rosemary leaves
and flowers for this dessert.
• You could also make 7.5cm/3in
circles of meringue instead of small
buttons and layer the soft fruit in
between circles of meringue.
• Use egg white powder as a substitute
for egg whites, if you like. It is high in
protein and low in fat, and means you
don't have to find a use for the egg
yolk, which is high in cholesterol.

TROPICAL FRUIT SALAD

A glorious medley of tropical fruits, and ginger to add that certain spice. Like all nuts, coconut is a significant source of fat, so go easy on the strips used for decoration.

INGREDIENTS

1 pineapple, about 600g/1lb 5oz
400g/14oz can guava halves in syrup
2 medium bananas, sliced
1 large mango, peeled, stoned and diced
*115g/4oz stem ginger, plus 30ml/2 tbsp of
the syrup from the jar*
60ml/4 tbsp thick coconut milk
10ml/2 tsp sugar
2.5ml/¹/2 tsp freshly grated nutmeg
2.5ml/¹/2 tsp ground cinnamon
a few fine strips of coconut, to decorate

SERVES 4–6

1 Peel, core and cube the pineapple, and place in a serving bowl. Drain the guavas, reserving the syrup, and chop. Add the guavas to the bowl with half the sliced banana and the mango.

2 Chop the stem ginger and add to the pineapple mixture.

3 Pour 30ml/2 tbsp of the ginger syrup, and the reserved guava syrup, into a blender or food processor. Add the remaining banana slices with the coconut milk and the sugar. Blend to a smooth, creamy purée.

NUTRITIONAL NOTES

Per portion:

Energy	340Kcals/1434kJ
Fat, total	1.8g
Saturated fat	0.83g
Cholesterol	0mg
Fibre	8.1g

4 Pour the banana and coconut mixture over the tropical fruit. Add a little grated nutmeg and a sprinkling of cinnamon on the top. Serve chilled, decorated with fine strips of coconut.

MELON AND STRAWBERRY SALAD

This colourful fruit salad can be served either as a dessert or as a refreshing appetizer.
Try to find three different colours of melon to serve.

INGREDIENTS

1 Galia melon

1 honeydew melon

1/2 watermelon

*225g/8oz/2 cups fresh strawberries,
halved if large*

15ml/1 tbsp lemon juice

15ml/1 tbsp clear honey

15ml/1 tbsp water

15ml/1 tbsp chopped fresh mint

SERVES 4

NUTRITIONAL NOTES

Per portion:

Energy	139Kcals/584kJ
Fat, total	0.84g
Saturated fat	0g
Cholesterol	0mg
Fibre	2g

1 Cut the melons in half and scrape out
the seeds. Use a melon baller to scoop out
the flesh, or use a knife to cut it into
cubes. Place the fruit in a serving bowl
and add the fresh strawberries.

COOK'S TIP

Make and prepare fresh for best taste.

2 Mix the lemon juice, honey and water
in a jug. Pour over the fruit and mix in.

3 Sprinkle the chopped mint over the
fruit and serve.

PAPAYA AND GREEN GRAPES WITH MINT SYRUP

Cool, fresh and virtually fat-free, this wonderful combination of textures and flavours makes the
perfect dessert to follow a spicy main course.

1 Peel the papaya. Discard the seeds. Cut
into small cubes. Cut the grapes in half.

2 In a bowl, mix together the lime juice,
grated root ginger, clear honey and
shredded mint leaves.

3 Add the papaya and grapes and toss
well. Cover and leave in a cool place to
marinate for 1 hour.

4 Serve in a large dish or individual
stemmed glasses, garnished with the
whole fresh mint leaves.

INGREDIENTS
2 large papayas
225g/8oz/2 cups seedless green grapes
juice of 3 limes
2.5cm/1in fresh root ginger, peeled
and grated
15ml/1 tbsp clear honey
5 fresh mint leaves, cut into thin strips,
plus extra whole leaves, to decorate

SERVES 4

NUTRITIONAL NOTES
Per portion:

Energy	120Kcals/507kJ
Fat, total	0.2g
Saturated fat	0g
Cholesterol	0mg
Fibre	4.4g

PAPAYA SKEWERS WITH PASSION FRUIT COULIS

Tropical fruits, full of natural sweetness, make a simple, exotic dessert.
If you are short of time the passion fruit flesh can be used without puréeing or sieving.

INGREDIENTS

3 ripe papayas
10 passion fruit or kiwi fruit
30ml/2 tbsp fresh lime juice
30ml/2 tbsp icing (confectioners') sugar
30ml/2 tbsp white rum
lime slices, to garnish

SERVES 6

NUTRITIONAL NOTES

Per portion:

Energy	94Kcals/399kJ
Fat, total	0.3g
Saturated fat	0g
Cholesterol	0mg
Fibre	4.1g

3 Press the fruit pulp through a sieve placed over a bowl; discard the seeds. Add the lime juice, icing sugar and rum, then stir the coulis well until the sugar has dissolved.

4 Spoon a little coulis on to plates and place the skewers on top. Scoop the flesh from the remaining passion fruit or kiwi fruit and spoon over. Garnish with slices of lime and serve at once.

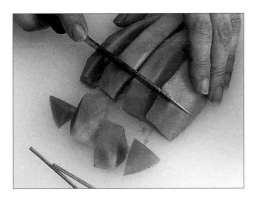

1 Cut the papayas in half and scoop out the seeds. Peel them and cut the flesh into even-size chunks. Thread the chunks on to six bamboo skewers.

2 Halve eight of the passion fruit or kiwi fruit and scoop out the flesh. Purée the flesh for a few seconds in a blender or food processor.

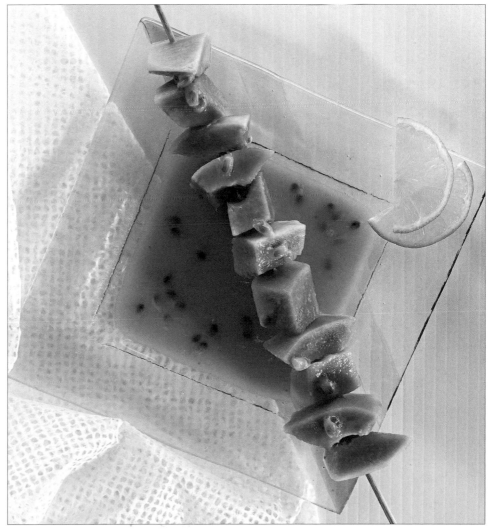

MIXED MELON SALAD

—

Several melon varieties are combined with strongly flavoured wild or woodland strawberries
for a delicious finale to a meal.

INGREDIENTS
1 cantaloupe or charentais melon
1 Galia melon
900g/2lb watermelon
175g/6oz wild strawberries
4 sprigs fresh mint

SERVES 4

1 Cut the cantaloupe and Galia melons
and watermelon in half.

2 Scoop out and discard the seeds from
the melons.

NUTRITIONAL NOTES
Per portion:

Energy	91Kcals/381kJ
Fat, total	0.7g
Saturated fat	0g
Cholesterol	0mg
Fibre	2.7g

3 Use a melon scoop, to remove the flesh
from the melons. Mix together in a bowl.
Cover and refrigerate for 2–3 hours.

4 Add the strawberries and mix lightly.
Spoon into four stemmed glass dishes.
Decorate with sprigs of mint.

THREE-FRUIT COMPOTE

Mixing dried fruits with fresh ones makes a good combination, especially when they are
flavoured delicately with a little orange-flower water.

INGREDIENTS
175g/6oz/1 cup ready-to-eat dried apricots
300ml/¹/₂ pint/1¹/₄ cups water
1 small ripe pineapple
1 small ripe melon, about 450g/1lb
15ml/1 tbsp orange-flower water
mint sprigs, to decorate

SERVES 6

NUTRITIONAL NOTES
Per portion:

Energy	86Kcals/360kJ
Fat, total	0.4g
Saturated fat	0g
Cholesterol	0mg
Fibre	3.2g

2 Peel and quarter the pineapple, then
cut the core from each quarter and
discard. Cut the flesh into chunks.

3 Cut the melon in half and scrape out
the seeds. Working over a bowl to
catch the juices, scoop balls from the
flesh. Tip the juices into the apricots.

4 Put the apricots, with the soaking
juices, into a bowl. Stir in the orange-
flower water. Add the pineapple and
melon and mix all the fruits gently.

5 Pour into a serving dish or individual
dessert dishes. Decorate with a mint sprig
and chill lightly before serving.

1 Put the apricots into a pan and pour
in the water. Bring to the boil, then lower
the heat and simmer for 5 minutes.
Leave to cool.

VARIATION
For a delicious red fruit salad, try
berry fruits with sliced plums, or for
green fruits, try apple, kiwi fruit and
green grapes.

SUMMER FRUIT SALAD ICE CREAM

What could be more cooling on a hot summer day than fresh summer fruits, lightly frozen in this irresistible ice?

INGREDIENTS

900g/2lb/6 cups mixed soft summer fruit,
such as raspberries, strawberries,
blackcurrants or redcurrants
2 eggs
250ml/8fl oz/1 cup low-fat Greek
(US strained plain) yogurt
175ml/6fl oz/3/4 cup red grape juice
15ml/1 tbsp powdered gelatine

SERVES 6

1 Reserve half the fruit for the decoration; purée the rest in a food processor, then sieve it over a bowl to make a smooth purée.

VARIATION

Use other fruit combinations such as apricots, peaches and nectarines, with apple or orange juice.

NUTRITIONAL NOTES
Per portion:

Energy	116Kcals/489kJ
Fat, total	3.9g
Saturated fat	1.69g
Cholesterol	66.8mg
Fibre	3.6g

2 Separate the eggs and whisk the yolks and the yogurt into the fruit purée.

3 Heat the grape juice until almost boiling, then remove it from the heat.

4 Sprinkle the gelatine over the grape juice and stir to dissolve the gelatine.

5 Whisk the dissolved gelatine mixture into the fruit purée. Cool, then pour the mixture into a container that can safely be used in the freezer. Freeze until half-frozen and slushy in consistency.

6 Whisk the egg whites in a grease-free bowl until stiff. Quickly fold them into the half-frozen mixture.

7 Return the ice cream to the freezer and freeze until almost firm. Scoop into individual dishes and decorate with the reserved soft fruits.

KEY LIME SORBET

Cool and refreshing, this traditional American sorbet is ideal for serving after a curry
or similar hot or spicy main course.

INGREDIENTS

275g/10oz/1¹/4 cups sugar
600ml/1 pint/2¹/2 cups water
grated rind of 1 lime
175ml/6fl oz/³/4 cup fresh lime juice
15ml/1 tbsp fresh lemon juice
30ml/2 tbsp icing (confectioners') sugar
lime shreds, to decorate

SERVES 4

1 In a small heavy pan, dissolve the sugar
in the water, without stirring, over
medium heat. When the sugar has
dissolved, boil the syrup for 5–6 minutes.
Remove from the heat and leave to cool.

2 Mix the cooled sugar syrup and lime
rind and juice in a jug or bowl. Stir well.
Sharpen the flavour by adding the
lemon juice.

3 Stir in the icing sugar until
well combined.

4 Freeze the mixture in an ice-cream
maker, following the manufacturer's
instructions. Decorate with lime shreds.

NUTRITIONAL NOTES
Per portion:

Energy	300Kcals/1278kJ
Fat, total	0g
Saturated fat	0g
Cholesterol	0mg
Fibre	0g

COOK'S TIP

If you do not have an ice-cream maker,
pour the mixture into a metal or plastic
freezer container and freeze until softly
set, about 3 hours. Remove from the
container and chop roughly. Process in
a food processor until smooth. Return
the mixture to the freezer container and
freeze again until set. Repeat this
process 2 or 3 times, until a smooth
consistency is obtained.

RASPBERRY SORBET

This stunning fresh fruit and herb garnish creates a bold border for the scoops of sorbet.
Make the sorbet in an ice-cream maker, if you have one.

INGREDIENTS
175g/6oz/³/4 cup caster (superfine) sugar
250ml/8fl oz/1 cup water
450g/1lb fresh or thawed
frozen raspberries
strained juice of 1 orange

FOR THE DECORATION
fresh flowers
a handful of strawberries or other
soft berries per serving

SERVES 8

1 Heat the caster sugar with the water in a pan, until dissolved. Bring to the boil, then set aside to cool.

2 Purée the raspberries with the orange juice, then press through a sieve to remove any seeds.

3 Mix the sugar syrup with the puréed raspberries

4 Pour or spoon the liquid into a freezer-proof container. Freeze for 2 hours or until ice crystals form around the edges. Whisk until smooth, then return to the freezer for 4 hours.

5 About 30 minutes before serving, transfer the sorbet to the refrigerator to soften slightly. Serve with halved strawberries and decorated with a flower, if you like.

NUTRITIONAL NOTES
Per portion:

Energy	158Kcals/669kJ
Fat, total	0.4g
Saturated fat	0g
Cholesterol	0mg
Fibre	3.4g

MANGO SORBET WITH MANGO SAUCE

—

After a heavy meal, this Indian speciality makes a very refreshing dessert. Remove from the
freezer 10 minutes before serving to allow it to soften and give the full flavour time to develop.

INGREDIENTS
900g/2lb/5 cups mango pulp
2.5ml/¹/2 tsp lemon juice
grated rind of 1 orange and 1 lemon
4 egg whites
50g/2oz/¹/4 cup caster (superfine) sugar
*120ml/4fl oz/¹/2 cup low-fat Greek
(US strained plain) yogurt*
*50g/2oz/¹/2 cup icing (confectioners')
sugar*

SERVES 4

1 In a large, chilled freezer-proof bowl,
mix half of the mango pulp with the
lemon juice and the grated citrus rind.

NUTRITIONAL NOTES
Per portion:

Energy	259Kcals/1090kJ
Fat, total	1.7g
Saturated fat	0.79g
Cholesterol	1.8mg
Fibre	5.9g

2 Whisk the egg whites in a clean,
grease-free bowl until soft peaks form,
then fold into the mango mixture, with the
sugar. Cover and freeze for at least 1 hour.

3 Remove the sorbet from the freezer and
beat again. Transfer to an ice-cream
container, and freeze until solid.

4 Lightly whisk the yogurt with the icing
sugar and the remaining mango pulp.
Spoon into a bowl and chill for 24 hours.
Scoop out individual servings of sorbet
and cover each with mango sauce.

LYCHEE AND ELDERFLOWER SORBET

The flavour of elderflowers is famous for bringing out the essence of gooseberries, but what is less well known is how wonderfully it complements lychees.

INGREDIENTS
175g/6oz/³/4 cup caster (superfine) sugar
400ml/14fl oz/1²/3 cups water
500g/1¹/4 lb fresh lychees, peeled
and stoned
15ml/1 tbsp elderflower cordial
dessert biscuits, to serve (optional)

SERVES 4

NUTRITIONAL NOTES
Per portion:

Energy	249Kcals/1058kJ
Fat, total	0.1g
Saturated fat	0g
Cholesterol	0mg
Fibre	0.9g

1 Gently heat the sugar and water in a small pan until the sugar has dissolved. Then boil the liquid for 5 minutes.

2 Add the lychees to the pan. Lower the heat and simmer for 7 minutes. Remove from the heat and allow to cool.

3 Purée the fruit and syrup, then pass it through a sieve, pressing with a spoon.

4 Stir the elderflower cordial into the strained purée.

5 Pour the mixture into a freezer-proof container. Freeze for 3 hours or until ice crystals start to form around the edges.

6 Remove the sorbet from the freezer and process briefly in a food processor or blender to break up the crystals. Repeat this process twice more, then freeze until firm.

7 Just before serving, transfer the sorbet to the refrigerator for 10 minutes to soften it slightly. Serve in scoops. with crisp dessert biscuits, if you like.

BLACKCURRANT SORBET

Blackcurrants make a vibrant and intensely flavoured sorbet. If not serving immediately, cover the sorbet tightly and freeze it again, for up to 1 week.

INGREDIENTS

100g/3¹/₂ oz/scant ¹/₂ cup caster (superfine) sugar
120ml/4fl oz/¹/₂ cup water
450g/1lb/4 cups blackcurrants
juice of ¹/₂ lemon
15ml/1 tbsp egg white

SERVES 4

1 Gently heat the sugar and water in a pan, stirring until the sugar dissolves. Boil the syrup for 2 minutes. Remove the pan from the heat and set aside to cool.

2 Remove the blackcurrants from the stalks by pulling them through the tines of a fork. Wash thoroughly. Reserve a few blackcurrants for the decoration.

3 In a food processor, process the blackcurrants and lemon juice until smooth. Alternatively, chop the blackcurrants coarsely, then add the lemon juice. Stir in the sugar syrup.

4 Press the purée through a sieve to remove the seeds.

5 Pour the blackcurrant purée into a non-metallic freezer-proof container. Cover with clear film or a lid and freeze until nearly firm, but still slushy.

6 Cut the sorbet into pieces and process in a food processor until smooth. With the machine running, add the egg white and process until well mixed.

7 Tip the sorbet back into the dish and freeze until almost firm. Chop the sorbet again and process until smooth. Serve immediately, decorated with blackcurrants.

NUTRITIONAL NOTES
Per portion:

Energy	132Kcals/558kJ
Fat, total	0g
Saturated fat	0g
Cholesterol	0mg
Fibre	4.1g

MANGO AND LIME SORBET IN LIME SIIELLS

—

This richly flavoured sorbet looks pretty served in the lime shells, but is also good
served in scoops for a more traditional presentation.

INGREDIENTS
4 large limes
1 ripe mango
7.5ml/1½ tsp powdered gelatine
2 egg whites
15ml/1 tbsp caster (superfine) sugar
strips of pared lime rind, to decorate

SERVES 4

1 Slice the top and bottom off each lime.
Squeeze the juice, keeping the shells
intact, then scrape out the shell membrane.

2 Halve, stone, peel and chop the mango.
Purée the flesh in a food processor with
30ml/2 tbsp of the lime juice.

3 Sprinkle the gelatine over 45ml/3 tbsp
of the lime juice in a small heatproof
bowl. Set aside until spongy, then place
the bowl in a pan of hot water, stirring
occasionally until the gelatine has
dissolved. Stir it into the mango mixture.

4 Whisk the egg whites in a grease-
free bowl until they hold soft peaks.
Whisk in the sugar. Fold the egg white
mixture quickly into the mango mixture.
Spoon the sorbet into the lime shells.
Any leftover sorbet can be frozen in
small ramekins.

NUTRITIONAL NOTES
Per portion:

Energy	83Kcals/350kJ
Fat, total	0.4g
Saturated fat	0g
Cholesterol	0mg
Fibre	2.3g

5 Place the filled shells in the freezer
until the sorbet is firm. Overwrap the
shells in clear film. Before serving, allow
the shells to stand at room temperature
for about 10 minutes; decorate them with
knotted strips of pared lime rind.

WATERMELON SORBET

A slice of this refreshing sorbet is the perfect way to cool down on a hot sunny day.
Ensure the watermelon is perfectly ripe when buying.

INGREDIENTS

1/2 small watermelon, about 1kg/2 1/4 lb
75g/3oz/6 tbsp caster (superfine) sugar
60ml/4 tbsp unsweetened cranberry
juice or water
30ml/2 tbsp lemon juice
sprigs of fresh mint, to decorate

SERVES 6

1 Cut the watermelon into six equal-size wedges. Scoop out the pink flesh, discarding the seeds but reserving the shell.

2 Select a bowl that is about the same size as the melon and which can safely be used in the freezer. Line it with clear film.

3 Arrange the melon skins in the bowl to re-form the shell, fitting them together snugly so that there are no gaps. Put in the freezer.

4 Mix the sugar and cranberry juice or water in a pan and stir over a low heat until the sugar dissolves. Bring to the boil, then lower the heat and simmer for 5 minutes. Leave the sugar syrup to cool.

5 Put the melon flesh and lemon juice in a blender and process to a smooth purée. Stir in the sugar syrup and pour into a non-metallic freezer-proof container. Freeze for 3–3 1/2 hours, or until it has a slushy texture.

6 Tip the sorbet into a chilled bowl and whisk to break up the ice crystals. Return to the freezer for another 30 minutes, whisk again, then tip into the melon shell and freeze until solid.

7 Remove the sorbet-filled melon shell from the freezer and carefully turn it upside down. Use a sharp knife to separate the segments, then quickly place them on individual plates. Decorate with mint sprigs and serve.

NUTRITIONAL NOTES
Per portion:

Energy	125Kcals/525kJ
Fat, total	0.52g
Saturated fat	0g
Cholesterol	0mg
Fibre	0.26g

COOK'S TIP
Watermelon seeds make a delicious and nutritious snack if toasted in a moderate oven until brown and hulled to remove the outer shell.

ORANGE ICE WITH STRAWBERRIES

Juicy oranges and really ripe strawberries make a flavoursome ice that does not need
any additional sweetening.

INGREDIENTS

6 large juicy oranges
350g/12oz/3 cups ripe strawberries
finely pared strips of orange rind,
to decorate

SERVES 4

NUTRITIONAL NOTES

Per portion:

Energy	124Kcals/518kJ
Fat, total	0.4g
Saturated fat	0g
Cholesterol	0mg
Fibre	5.6g

1 Squeeze the juice from the oranges and
pour into a shallow freezer-proof bowl.
Place the bowl in the freezer.

2 When ice crystals form around the edge
beat the mixture thoroughly. Repeat at
30-minute intervals over a 4-hour period.

3 Halve the strawberries and arrange
them on a serving plate.

4 Scoop the ice into serving glasses,
decorate with strips of orange rind and
serve immediately with the strawberries.

COOK'S TIP

The ice will keep for up to 3 weeks in
the freezer. Sweet ruby grapefruits or
deep red blood oranges can be used for
a different flavour and colour.

INDEX